Progressive Farmer

Country Living Recipes 1980

JEAN WICKSTROM LILES

Oxmoor House, Inc.
Birmingham

Copyright © 1980 by Oxmoor House, Inc.
Book Division of Southern Progress Corporation
P.O. Box 2463, Birmingham, Alabama 35201

Eugene Butler   Chairman of the Board
Emory Cunningham   President and Publisher
Vernon Owens, Jr.   Executive Vice President

Conceived, edited and published by Oxmoor House, Inc., under the
direction of:

Don Logan   Vice President and General Manager
Gary McCalla   Editor, *Southern Living*
C.G. Scruggs   Editor, *Progressive Farmer*
John Logue   Editor-in-Chief
John Floyd   Coordinator, *Southern Country Living* Section,
                                       Progressive Farmer
Jean Wickstrom Liles   Foods Editor, *Progressive Farmer*
Ann H. Harvey   Managing Editor
Jerry Higdon   Production Manager

Progressive Farmer Country Living Recipes 1980

Associate Production Manager: Joan Denman
Assistant Editors: Susan Payne, Annette Thompson
Designer: Faith Nance
Food Illustrator: Thomas F. Ford
Photographers: Jerome Drown: cover; John O'Hagan: pages i, 14,
    34, 62; Charles Walton: pages 13, 24, 33, 51, 72, 89, 90

Progressive Farmer Foods Staff: Rebecca Brennan,
    Margaret Chason, Jane Elliott, Martha Hinrichs, Diane Hogan,
    Beverly Morrow, Karen Parker, Peggy Smith, Donna Taylor,
    Linda Welch

Progressive Farmer and *Southern Country Living* are federally
registered trademarks belonging to Progressive Farmer, Inc.,
Birmingham, Alabama.

ISBN: 0–8487–0514–9

Manufactured in the United States of America
First Printing 1980

Cover: *Here's a sampling of simple, but delicious,
cooking: Chicken Pie with Sweet Potato Crust (page
45), Never-Fail Pan Rolls (page 31), Milky Way
Cake (page 74), Deep-Dish Apple Pie (page 85), and
Spiced Peaches (page 106).*

Page i: *Selecting fresh, tender spinach is the first step
to making a perfect Spinach Soufflé (page 103).*

Page ii: *Autumn brings colorful trees and a bounty of
pecans to use in a variety of recipes.*

Contents

Author's Note

Old-fashioned home cooking has long been a symbol of hospitality in the South. From our country kitchens come treasured recipes that are unequaled and unexcelled in other regions. When many think of Southern foods, images of country ham, turnip greens, and cornbread come to mind. They are favorites, but Southern food is more—much more. From chicken pie to barbecued ribs, the food of the South is as varied as its people.

Country Living Recipes *is our proud collection of every recipe appearing in* Progressive Farmer *during 1980 plus over 100 favorite classic recipes selected from previous issues of the magazine.*

Each month the South's best cooks favor us with hundreds of their family's favorite recipes. Handed down from generation to generation, these recipes have already passed a taste test in country kitchens throughout the South. Prior to publication, these recipes are tested, tasted, and evaluated by our staff of experienced home economists. Several factors are considered in our recipe evaluation: taste, appearance, ease of preparation, and cost of dish. We believe this procedure ensures the standard of excellence our readers have grown to expect from Progressive Farmer.

But Country Living Recipes *is more than just a recipe book. For instance, our Canning and Freezing Guide will assist you in savoring year-round the fruits and vegetables from your garden.*

Since Southerners still take time to enjoy cooking and entertaining in their homes, we've planned a special Home Entertaining Guide emphasizing ideas for everything from planning a menu to serving the meal. This chapter even includes sixteen complete menus built around recipes in Country Living Recipes.

We believe you will find these recipes appealing to the varied tastes and interests of Southerners. Country Living Recipes *is not only for the experienced cook but for the novice as well. It is for cooks everywhere who are searching for new ways to please the appetites of family and friends. We trust this will become your most practical and usable cookbook.*

Jean Wickstrom Liles

Canning and Freezing Guide

One of the advantages of summer is the abundance of fresh fruits and vegetables from our gardens. Modern canning and freezing techniques let us preserve the foods for year-round enjoyment.

Canning allows preservation of large quantities of food with no special storage equipment required other than standard containers. Freezing is a quick method of preservation that keeps maximum color, flavor, and nutrients, but storage is limited to freezer space available. Whichever method you choose, follow the up-to-date guidelines in this chapter to ensure safe storage of the food.

Canning

Canning fresh fruits and vegetables while they are in peak supply is not only economical but also gives you a feeling of true accomplishment. In addition, the convenience of having a variety of home-canned foods to select from is unbeatable.

Canning is a food preservation process in which all organisms that might cause food spoilage are destroyed by heating food to a specific temperature for a certain length of time. Too, enzyme action is stopped at the peak of the food's maturity, thus preserving flavor and nutritive value.

General Canning Procedures

The boiling-water-bath method is used for processing acid foods, such as fruits, tomatoes (with high-acid content), pickled vegetables, and sauerkraut. These acid foods are canned safely at boiling temperatures in a water-bath canner.

The steam-pressure method is used for processing low-acid foods, such as meats, fish, poultry, and most vegetables. A temperature higher than boiling is required to can these foods safely. In this method, the food is processed in a steam-pressure canner at 10 pounds pressure (240°) to ensure that all of the spoilage microorganisms are destroyed.

Selecting Containers: Jars not made especially for home canning are not recommended for use in canning foods that must be processed in boiling water or with steam. Reserve these jars for canning foods in which pressure and temperature requirements are lower, such as jellies, jams, and preserves.

Standard glass jars made especially for home canning vary in size and type. The specially designed lids ensure a complete seal. Glass jars are usually sealed with a two-piece cap consisting of a flat metal lid with a rubbery sealing compound around the edge and a threaded metal band that screws over the flat lid to hold it securely. The threaded bands for this type closure may be used several times, but the flat lids should be purchased for each canning season to ensure perfect seals.

Another type closure for glass jars is the porcelain-lined zinc cap with shoulder rubber ring. Porcelain-lined zinc caps may be reused as long as they are in good condition; the rubber rings should not be reused. Have clean new rubber rings of the correct size for each canning season; unused ones from last year may have deteriorated. Do not test rings by stretching.

Be sure to check all containers before using. Discard any with chips, cracks, rust, or dents, since defects prevent an airtight seal.

Wash jars and closures in hot soapy water; rinse well. Put jars in hot water until ready to fill. Follow manufacturer's directions for boiling metal lids; some require only a short period in hot water.

Packing and Sealing Jars: Before processing, food is packed into jars by either the cold-pack (raw-pack) method or the hot-pack method. Cold pack means simply that the jars are filled with unheated or raw food and then covered with boiling water or other liquid to within ½ inch of the top of the jar. When this method is used, the food should be packed tightly in the containers because shrinkage will occur during processing.

In the hot-pack method, the jars are filled with hot or cooked food. The food should be packed rather loosely, within ½ to 1 inch of the top, and the jar filled with boiling liquid to within ½ inch of the top.

Whatever packing method is used, a certain amount of space must be left at the top of each jar. This headspace allows the food to expand during processing. The amount of headspace varies with the type of food being processed and the jar size. In general, leave ½-inch headspace in jars when packing fruits and non-starchy vegetables; leave 1-inch headspace for starchy vegetables and meats.

All air bubbles must be removed before sealing the jars. Run a rubber spatula or knife gently between the jar and the food. For solid packs (corn, greens, mashed pumpkin) remove the air bubbles by cutting through the center several times. Add more liquid, if necessary, to cover packed food. If not completely covered, the food at the top of the jar may darken.

Wipe off the rim of the jar with a paper towel or clean cloth. Put the cap on each jar as soon as it is packed. When using jars with metal screw bands and flat metal lid closures, put the flat lid on with the sealing compound next to the jar top. Screw the metal band as tight as you can by hand. When the band is tight, the closure allows air to escape during processing and at the same time seals tightly as the jars are removed from the processing canner. Never tighten screw bands after removing jars from the canner as this breaks the seal. Remove screw bands after jars cool since they often rust and become difficult to loosen.

If you are using a jar with a porcelain-lined zinc cap, fit the wet rubber ring down on the jar shoulder, stretching the ring as little as possible. Pack the jar, leaving the recommended headspace. Wipe rubber ring and jar rim clean. Screw cap on firmly; then turn back ¼ inch. As soon as the jar is removed from the canner, screw cap on tightly to complete the seal.

Cooling and Storing: To prevent overcooking after processing, remove jars from waterbath canner immediately; wait until pressure is zero in steam-pressure canner before removing jars. Place the jars upright on a rack, folded cloth, or a wooden cutting board. Allow enough room between jars for air circulation, but avoid drafts.

There may be a popping sound as jars with metal lids cool; this means that the flat lid is settling onto the top of the jar and also that you have a good seal. When jars are cool, test the seal by running your fingertip over the top of the lid. If the lid curves downward, the seal is good. Remove screw bands before storing.

To test the seal on jars with porcelain-lined caps, turn each jar partly over in your hands and check for leakage.

If any jar fails to seal after processing,

either repack and reprocess or refrigerate the jars and use the contents as soon as possible.

Canned foods should be labeled to show contents and date, then stored in a cool, dry, dark place. If the jars have a good seal and are properly stored, the food should retain flavor and color for a year.

Boiling-Water-Bath Canning

Fruits, tomatoes (with high-acid content), pickled vegetables, rhubarb, and sauerkraut—all high in acid content—should be processed by the boiling-water-bath method. Follow the directions in General Canning Procedures for selecting containers, packing and sealing the jars, cooling, and storing.

Equipment: A water-bath canner is simply a large metal container with a tight-fitting lid. Specially designed water-bath canners are available in 7- to 9-quart sizes and can be purchased in most large hardware stores.

The canner must be deep enough to allow space for water to boil freely over and around each jar. (Allow 2 to 4 inches above jar tops for brisk boiling.) The canner must have a wire or wooden rack so that the jars do not sit directly on the bottom of the canner. The rack permits water to circulate freely under the jars during processing.

If a steam-pressure canner is deep enough, it may be used for the boiling-water-bath method. Cover the canner, but do not fasten the lid; leave the petcock (vent) open so that steam may escape as the water boils.

Preparation of Food: Choose fresh, firm, fully ripened fruits and vegetables. Process as soon after picking as possible. If a delay is unavoidable, store the food in a cool, airy place. Sort fruits and vegetables according to size and ripeness for more even cooking; handle gently to avoid bruising.

Since dirt carries bacteria that is often difficult to destroy, wash fruits and vegetables thoroughly. It is best to wash small amounts at a time under running water. Avoid letting fruits and vegetables soak in water; they may lose flavor and food value.

If the fruit or vegetable is to be peeled before canning, dip it first in boiling water then quickly in cold water. This enables the skins to be slipped off easily. If the fruit is not peeled, prick the skin in several places with a needle. This will not prevent cracking, but it does keep the skins from bursting during processing.

Some fruits, such as apples, apricots, peaches, and pears, have light-colored flesh that darkens very quickly after being peeled. To prevent discoloration, drop the fruit as it is peeled into a mixture of 1 gallon water, 2 tablespoons lemon juice or vinegar, and 2 tablespoons salt; do not allow fruit to soak longer than 20 minutes. Since the mixture may affect the flavor of the fruit, rinse fruit thoroughly before packing into jars. Commercial ascorbic-citric mixtures are also available to prevent discoloration; use as directed on the label.

Sugar helps canned fruits retain their shape, color, and flavor. But since sugar is not needed to prevent spoilage, the fruit may be canned in its own juice or in water. When sugar is used, it is usually added to the fruit in syrup form.

To make sugar syrup, measure sugar (or a mixture of sugar and corn syrup or honey) and water into a saucepan; heat until sugar dissolves. Keep syrup hot until needed. For each pint of fruit, allow ⅔ cup syrup; for each quart, allow 1 to 1½ cups syrup. The density of the syrup will vary according to the fruit to be canned. Follow this formula to make sugar syrup:

Type Of Syrup	Sugar (Cups)	Water (Cups)	Yield (Cups)
Light	2	4	5
Medium	3	4	5½
Heavy	4¾	4	6½

—Medium syrup made with corn syrup: 1½ cups sugar and 1 cup syrup to 3 cups water
—Medium syrup made with honey: 1 cup sugar and 1 cup honey to 4 cups water

Pack and seal the jars as directed in General Canning Procedures.

Processing: These steps are a guide to processing by the boiling-water-bath canning method.

1) Set water-bath canner on range; fill half full of water. Place cover on canner, and start heating water over high heat. Water should be hot but not boiling for cold pack and boiling for hot pack.

2) Arrange packed jars on rack so they do not touch the sides of the canner or each other. Add enough boiling water to cover top of jars with 1 to 2 inches of water. Be careful not to pour water directly on jars.

3) Cover canner; begin counting the processing time when water comes to a full rolling boil. Lower heat, but maintain a steady, gentle boil for the recommended length of time. Be sure that water covers the jars at all times during processing.

4) Cool and store as directed in General Canning Procedures.

Yield: The exact yield of canned fruits from a given quantity of fresh fruits depends upon the quality and the freshness of the fruits, their maturity, and the method by which the particular fruits are packed.

Fruit	Pounds Raw To Yield 1 Quart Canned
Apples	2½ to 3
Berries (except strawberries)	1½ to 3
Peaches	2 to 3
Pears	2 to 3
Plums	1½ to 2½
Tomatoes	2½ to 3½

Steam-Pressure Canning

Steam-pressure canning is the procedure used for canning low-acid foods—all meats, poultry, fish, and most vegetables. Follow the directions in General Canning Procedures for selecting containers, packing and sealing the jars, cooling, and storing.

Equipment: A steam-pressure canner consists of a heavy metal kettle with a cover that can be clamped or locked down to make the kettle airtight. Although pressure canners vary slightly (and the manufacturer's directions should be followed carefully for the brand you are using), their essential features are similar. The controls include a petcock, which allows air to be driven out and the canner to be filled with steam; a safety valve to allow steam to escape if the pressure becomes too high (in some models the safety valve and petcock are one unit); and a gauge that registers pressure within the cooker. The canner has a rack to keep jars from touching the bottom of the canner.

Preparation of Food: Vegetables to be canned should be fresh, young, and tender, yet full flavored and firm enough to retain their shape during processing. Wash in several changes of cold water, lifting vegetables out of the water so that dirt is not rinsed over them. Scrub root vegetables with a brush. Sort vegetables for size and ripeness to ensure even cooking; handle carefully to prevent bruising.

Pack and seal the jars as instructed in General Canning Procedures.

Processing: Be sure to follow the manufacturer's directions for using your particular canner (especially with regard to closing the canner). The procedures described here will serve as a general guide to processing by the steam-pressure method.

1) Set canner on the range. Pour 2 or 3 inches boiling water or the amount recommended by the manufacturer in the canner. Arrange packed jars on the rack so that they are not touching. If you have two layers of jars in the canner, use a rack between each layer, and stagger the jars on the upper rack.

2) Cover the canner, and lock securely according to directions given for your canner. Place over high heat. Be sure no steam escapes except through the petcock (vent) or weighted gauge opening on the top of the canner.

3) Watch until steam pours out of the petcock in a steady stream. Let steam escape steadily for 10 minutes to allow air to escape from the canner. Then close petcock or weighted gauge.

4) Let pressure rise to 10 pounds (240°). The moment this pressure is reached, start counting the processing time. Keep pressure

constant by regulating the heat under the canner. Do not lower pressure by opening the petcock; do not allow a draft to blow on the canner. When the processing time is up, remove canner from heat immediately.

5) Let the canner stand until pressure registers zero. Do not run water over canner or rush cooling. Wait a minute or two; then release steam very slowly or remove weighted gauge slowly so that liquid is not drawn from the jars. Unlatch and remove the lid, tilting it away from your face to avoid steam burns.

6) Cool and store as directed in General Canning Procedures.

Yield: The yield of canned vegetables from a given quantity of fresh vegetables depends upon the quality and freshness of the vegetables, their maturity, and the method by which the vegetables are packed.

Vegetables	Pounds Raw To Yield 1 Quart Canned
Beans, Green	1½ to 2½
Beans, Lima (in pods)	3 to 5
Beets	2½ to 3½
Carrots	2 to 3
Corn (in husks)	3 to 6
Okra	1½
Peas, English (in pods)	3 to 6
Squash, Pumpkin and Winter	1½ to 3
Squash, Summer	2 to 4
Sweet Potatoes	2 to 3

BERRIES (EXCEPT STRAWBERRIES)

Select fully ripened berries. Handle as little as possible. Wash and cap berries; drain well.

Hot Pack: (Use for blackberries and others that hold their shape well.) Add ½ cup sugar to each 4 cups berries; cook until sugar dissolves and mixture comes to a boil, stirring gently to keep berries from sticking. Pack berries into jars, leaving ½-inch headspace. (If there is not enough syrup to cover berries, add boiling water, leaving ½-inch headspace.) Cover at once with metal lids, and screw metal bands tight. Process pints for 10 minutes and quarts for 15 minutes in boiling-water bath.

Cold Pack: (Use for red raspberries or others that do not hold their shape well.) Make a medium syrup: Combine 3 cups sugar and 1 quart water; cook until sugar dissolves. Yield will be 5½ cups. It usually takes 1 to 1½ cups syrup for each quart of fruit. Pack raw berries into jars, leaving ½-inch headspace. Shake jars as berries are added to get a full pack. Cover with boiling syrup, leaving ½-inch headspace. Cover at once with metal lids, and screw metal bands tight. Process pints for 15 minutes and quarts for 20 minutes in boiling-water bath.

PEACHES

Select ripe, firm peaches. Peel and cut into halves or slices. Remove pits. To prevent fruit from darkening, use an ascorbic-citric mixture according to the directions, or drop peach slices into a mild salt solution (2 tablespoons salt and 2 tablespoons vinegar or lemon juice per gallon of water). If using salt solution, rinse and drain fruit before packing.

Make a Medium Syrup: Combine 3 cups sugar and 1 quart water; heat until sugar dissolves. Yield will be 5½ cups. Usually 1 to 1½ cups of syrup are needed for each quart of fruit.

Hot Pack: Heat peaches in hot syrup. Pack peaches into jars, leaving ½-inch headspace. Cover with boiling syrup, leaving ½-inch headspace. Cover with metal lids; screw metal bands tight. Process pints for 20 minutes and quarts for 25 minutes in boiling-water bath.

Cold Pack: Pack raw peaches into jars, leaving ½-inch headspace. Cover with boiling syrup, leaving ½-inch headspace. Cover at once with metal lids, and screw metal bands tight. Process pints for 25 minutes and quarts for 30 minutes in boiling-water bath.

APPLE BUTTER

2 dozen apples (about 6 pounds)
2 quarts fresh apple cider
3 cups sugar
1½ teaspoons ground cinnamon
½ teaspoon ground cloves

Core and slice apples (do not peel). Place apples and cider in a large kettle; cook until tender. Press apples through a sieve or food mill (should yield about 3 quarts pulp).

Cook pulp until thick enough to round up in a spoon, stirring frequently to prevent sticking. Add sugar and spices. Cook mixture over low heat about 1 hour, stirring frequently, until thickened.

Pour immediately into hot sterilized jars, leaving ¼-inch headspace. Place lids on jars, and screw bands tight. Process in boiling-water bath for 10 minutes. Yield: about 5 pints.

CARROT JAM

8 cups shredded carrots
6 cups sugar
Grated rind and juice of 4 lemons
1 teaspoon ground cloves
1 teaspoon ground allspice
1 teaspoon ground cinnamon

Combine all ingredients in a large Dutch oven; stir well. Bring to a slow boil, reduce heat, and simmer 15 minutes, stirring constantly. Quickly pour jam into hot sterilized jars, leaving ¼-inch headspace; cover at once with metal lids, and screw metal bands tight. Process 10 minutes in boiling-water bath. Yield: about 6 cups.

GRAPE JELLY

2 cups bottled unsweetened grape juice
3½ cups sugar
1 (3-ounce) package liquid fruit pectin

Combine grape juice and sugar in a large Dutch oven; bring to a boil, stirring constantly. Stir in fruit pectin; return to a boil and continue boiling an additional minute, stirring constantly. Remove from heat and skim off foam with a metal spoon.

Quickly pour jelly into sterilized jars, leaving ½-inch headspace. Cover at once with an ⅛-inch layer of paraffin. Cover with lids. Yield: 4 cups.

PEACH CONSERVE

5 pounds underripe peaches, peeled and sliced
Grated rind of 1 orange
3 oranges, peeled and sectioned
7 cups sugar
¾ pound blanched almonds, cut lengthwise into halves or slivers

Combine all ingredients except almonds in a Dutch oven; bring to a boil, stirring occasionally, until sugar dissolves. Boil gently 45 minutes, stirring frequently. Stir in almonds; cook an additional 10 minutes.

Quickly pour into hot sterilized jars, leaving ¼-inch headspace. Cover at once with metal lids, and screw metal bands tight. Process in boiling-water bath for 10 minutes. Yield: 4½ cups.

PEAR PRESERVES

3 cups sugar
2 cups water
8 cups peeled, cored, and coarsely chopped pears

Combine sugar and water in a large Dutch oven; bring mixture to a boil, stirring occasionally, until sugar dissolves.

Cook at a rolling boil 5 minutes. Add pears and simmer 1 to 1½ hours or until pears are transparent.

Quickly spoon pears into hot sterilized jars. If necessary, boil syrup 3 to 5 minutes longer or until thickened. Pour over fruit, leaving ¼-inch headspace. Cover at once with metal lids, and screw metal bands tight. Process in boiling-water bath 10 minutes. Yield: about 7 cups.

Aylene Ferguson,
Fall Branch, Tenn.

MIXED VEGETABLES

8 cups sugar
4 cups water
2 cups vinegar (5% acidity)
5 tablespoons celery seeds
5 tablespoons mustard seeds
2 tablespoons salt
5 quarts water
28 ears fresh corn, cut from cob (3 quarts)
2 quarts (2- to 3-inch) cucumbers
1 medium head cabbage, shredded
2 quarts lima beans (4 pounds)
1½ pounds celery, cut into 1-inch pieces
   (2 quarts)
2 quarts sliced carrots (3 pounds)
3 large onions, cut into eighths (1 quart)
3 large green tomatoes, cut into eighths
   (1 quart)

Combine sugar, 4 cups water, vinegar, celery seeds, mustard seeds, and salt in a large saucepan; bring mixture to a boil, stirring to dissolve sugar.

Bring 5 quarts water to a boil in a large canning kettle. Add all vegetables to water; stir gently to combine. Bring water to a second boil; boil 5 minutes.

Pack vegetables into hot, sterilized jars; pour syrup over vegetables, leaving 1-inch headspace. Cover at once with metal lids, and screw bands tight. Process in pressure canner at 10 pounds; 55 minutes for pints, 85 minutes for quarts. Yield: about 9 quarts. *Bertha Miller, Thomas, Okla.*

VEGETABLE SOUP

1½ quarts water
8 cups peeled, cored, chopped tomatoes
6 cups peeled, cubed potatoes
4 cups lima beans
4 cups cut corn, uncooked
6 cups sliced carrots
2 cups sliced celery
2 cups chopped onion
Salt

Combine water and vegetables; boil 5 minutes. Pour into hot jars, leaving 1-inch headspace. Add ¼ teaspoon salt to pints and ½ teaspoon to quarts. Cover at once with metal lids, and screw metal bands tight. Process in pressure canner at 10 pounds pressure (240°). Process pints for 55 minutes and quarts for 85 minutes. Yield: about 14 pints or 7 quarts.

WHOLE KERNEL CORN

Husk corn and remove silks; wash. Cut corn from cob at about two-thirds the depth of the kernel; do not scrape.

Hot Pack: Add 2 cups of boiling water to 4 cups of cut corn; boil 3 minutes. Pack corn in jars, leaving 1-inch headspace. Add ½ teaspoon salt to each pint, 1 teaspoon salt to each quart. Add boiling liquid, leaving 1-inch headspace. Cover at once with metal lids, and screw metal bands tight. Process in pressure canner at 10 pounds pressure (240°). Process pints for 55 minutes, quarts for 85 minutes.

Cold Pack: Pack corn in jars, leaving 1-inch headspace. Do not shake or press down. Add ½ teaspoon salt to each pint, 1 teaspoon to each quart. Cover with boiling water, leaving 1-inch headspace. Cover at once with metal lids, and screw metal bands tight. Process in pressure canner at 10 pounds pressure (240°). Process pints for 55 minutes, quarts for 85 minutes.

OKRA

Select young, tender pods of okra. Wash okra; trim stem ends. Cook for 1 minute in boiling water; drain. Leave pods whole or cut into 1-inch slices. Use hot-pack method only.

Hot Pack: Pack okra into jars, leaving ½-inch headspace. Add ½ teaspoon salt to pints and 1 teaspoon to quarts. Cover with boiling water, leaving ½-inch headspace. Cover at once with metal lids, and screw metal bands tight. Process in pressure canner at 10 pounds pressure (240°). Process pints for 25 minutes and quarts for 40 minutes.

CRISP SWEET DILL PICKLES

About 2½ gallons cucumbers, sliced
 lengthwise
2 cups pickling salt
1 tablespoon pickling lime
10 cups vinegar (5% acidity)
8 cups sugar, divided
16 large fresh dill sprigs

Place cucumbers in a large crock. Combine 1 gallon water and salt in a large kettle; bring to a boil and pour over cucumbers. Cover and weight down cucumbers. Let stand four days; remove scum daily.

Pour off salt water on fifth day, and add 1 gallon clear boiling water. Cover and weight down cucumbers; let stand 24 hours.

Drain cucumbers on sixth day. Combine 1 gallon water and pickling lime in a large kettle. Bring to a boil and pour over cucumbers. Cover as directed above and let stand 24 hours.

Drain cucumbers on seventh day, and cover with 1 gallon clear boiling water.

Drain cucumbers on eighth day. Combine vinegar and 5 cups sugar in a large kettle; bring to a boil. Add dill to cucumbers and pour boiling syrup over cucumbers. For the next three days, pour syrup into a large kettle, and add 1 cup sugar daily; reheat and pour over cucumbers. With the third heating, pack pickles into sterilized jars, leaving ½-inch headspace. Cover pickles with boiling syrup to within ½ inch of top. Adjust lids; screw bands tight. Process in boiling-water bath 5 minutes. Yield: about 8 quarts. *Bertha Miller,*
Thomas, Okla.

PICKLED OKRA

3 pounds small okra pods
6 small celery leaves
6 small hot peppers
6 small cloves garlic
1 tablespoon dillseeds, divided
2 cups white vinegar (4% to 6% acidity)
4 cups water
½ cup pickling salt

Remove part of stem from each okra pod. Firmly pack okra into hot sterilized jars. Place a celery leaf, pepper pod, and clove of garlic in each jar. Add ½ teaspoon dillseeds per jar.

Combine vinegar, water, and salt in a medium saucepan; bring to a boil. Pour over okra. Top with lids, and screw metal bands tight. Process in boiling-water bath for 10 minutes. Yield: 6 pints. *Varniece R. Warren,*
Hermitage, Ark.

HOMEMADE BARBECUE SAUCE

8 quarts (about 38 large) ripe tomatoes,
 peeled and coarsely chopped
2 cups chopped onion
2 cups sugar
1 cup firmly packed brown sugar
2 to 3 cups vinegar (5% acidity)
1 cup Worcestershire sauce
2 tablespoons salt
1 teaspoon ground allspice
2 tablespoons barbecue spice
2 tablespoons hot sauce
1 tablespoon celery seeds
2 teaspoons mustard seeds
2 (3½-inch) cinnamon sticks

Combine all ingredients in a kettle; cook over medium heat 2 to 3 hours or until thickened, stirring occasionally. Remove cinnamon.

Pour into hot sterilized jars, leaving ½-inch headspace. Adjust lids; process 15 minutes in a boiling-water bath. Yield: 4½ quarts.
 Brenda Thompson,
Anniston, Ala.

PICANTE SAUCE

10 ripe tomatoes peeled, cored, and quartered
1 large onion, quartered
1 small carrot, sliced
½ cup finely chopped jalapeño peppers
½ cup finely chopped chili peppers
¼ teaspoon pepper
1½ teaspoons pickling salt
1 tablespoon garlic salt

Place small amounts of tomato, onion, and carrot in container of an electric blender or processor; blend until finely chopped. Repeat.

Combine vegetables and remaining ingredients in a Dutch oven; cook over medium heat 30 minutes. Pour into hot sterilized jars, leaving ½-inch headspace. Adjust lids; process pints in pressure canner at 10 pounds pressure (240°) for 25 minutes. (Do not process in jars larger than pints.) Yield: 4½ pints.

Mrs. Jesse James,
Boise City, Okla.

HOTDOG RELISH

7 medium cucumbers, peeled and shredded
3 large onions, shredded
3 large green peppers, chopped
3 large red peppers, chopped
5 tablespoons salt
3 cups sugar
3½ cups water
1 cup vinegar (5% acidity)

Combine vegetables and salt in a large bowl. Cover and let stand overnight.

Drain thoroughly, pressing out excess liquid; rinse and drain. Add sugar, water, and vinegar; mix well. Pack into sterilized jars, leaving ½-inch headspace. Cover at once with metal lids, and screw bands tight. Process in boiling-water bath for 15 minutes. Yield: about 6 pints.

Bertha Miller,
Thomas, Okla.

SPICY TOMATO RELISH

4 quarts (about 18 large) tomatoes, peeled, cored, and chopped
1 large onion, chopped (about 2 cups)
2 medium-size green peppers, chopped
1½ cups sugar
1⅓ cups vinegar (5% acidity)
1 tablespoon salt
1 tablespoon celery seeds
1 teaspoon ground ginger
1 teaspoon ground cinnamon
1 teaspoon ground cloves
1 teaspoon ground allspice

Combine all ingredients in a large Dutch oven. Bring to a boil; reduce heat, and simmer 2½ hours or until mixture reaches desired thickness. Stir frequently.

Spoon relish into hot sterilized jars, leaving ½-inch headspace. Adjust lids; process 15 minutes in a boiling-water bath. Yield: 4 pints.

Barbara Dale Cable,
Mocksville, N.C.

STUFFED SWEET PEPPERS

About 3 dozen tomato peppers or 2 dozen red and green peppers
9 cups sugar
10½ cups water
3 cups vinegar (5% acidity)
2 tablespoons salt
Slaw (recipe follows)

Cut tops from peppers; remove membrane and seeds.

Combine sugar, water, vinegar, and salt in a large mixing bowl; stir until sugar is dissolved. Set aside.

Spoon slaw into peppers. Pack peppers tightly into hot, sterilized wide-mouth quart jars; pour syrup over peppers, leaving ½-inch headspace. Cover at once with metal lids, and screw bands tight. Process in boiling-water bath for 20 minutes. Yield: about 5 quarts.

Note: Amount of syrup needed will vary depending on how tightly peppers are packed and type of pepper. Tomato peppers are smaller and will pack more tightly, requiring less syrup than red and green peppers.

SLAW:
1½ cups sugar
½ cup vinegar (5% acidity)
½ cup water
1 teaspoon salt
10 cups shredded cabbage

Combine sugar, vinegar, water, and salt in a large mixing bowl; stir until sugar is dissolved. Stir cabbage into liquid mixture. Yield: about 4 quarts.

Bertha Miller,
Thomas, Okla.

Freezing

Of the many ways to preserve fresh fruits and vegetables, the best way to retain natural flavor is through freezing. Freezing also maintains nutritive quality well, and it's one of the simplest and quickest methods of food preservation available.

Remember that freezing does not improve an overripe, underripe, or otherwise inferior product. So select only the highest quality fresh fruits and vegetables that are at their peak of maturity.

General Directions For Freezing

Containers: Successful freezing depends heavily on the use of moisture-proof, vapor-proof packaging to keep the food's natural moisture from escaping. In addition to special freezer bags and cartons, glass, metal, and rigid plastic containers can be used. Suitable wrapping materials include heavy-duty aluminum foil and laminated freezer paper.

Packing and Storing: When filling containers, be sure to leave the amount of headspace for each size jar to allow for expansion of the food during freezing: ½ inch in wide-mouthed pint containers; 1 inch in wide-mouthed quart containers; ¾ inch in narrow-top pint containers; 1½ inches in narrow-top quart containers. And be sure to press out all excess air in plastic bags before fastening. Wrappings should be tightly molded to the food to prevent air pockets and taped securely with freezer tape.

After packing, label each item with the name of the food and the date. Place products frozen earliest in the front of the freezer so they will be used first.

Promptness in handling, processing, sealing, and freezing food is important, as it helps retain the quality of a product.

Most fruits and vegetables maintain high quality when frozen for 8 to 12 months; citrus products for 4 to 6 months. It's a good idea to post a list of frozen foods near the freezer and keep a record of when they were frozen.

Freezing Fruits

Most fruits, except bananas, can be frozen successfully. Select firm, ripe fruit that you would choose for eating. Then prepare it carefully for freezing, working with small quantities at a time.

Some fruits, such as peaches, pears, plums, figs, persimmons, and apples, discolor easily. Commercial ascorbic-citric mixtures are available to prevent this; use as directed on the label.

Fruits may be frozen in a sugar syrup, in sugar, or without any sugar at all.

Syrup Packs: These are generally used for firm fruits. Bring sugar and water to a boil, stirring until sugar dissolves. Chill thoroughly before combining with fruit. The following syrups are most often used:

Type Of Syrup	Sugar (Cups)	Water (Cups)	Yield (Cups)
30%	2	4	5
35%	2½	4	5⅓
40%	3	4	5½
50%	4¾	4	6¼

Syrup should completely cover the fruit in the freezer container. Crumpled moisture-proof, vapor-proof paper can be placed between the lid and the fruit to keep the fruit submerged. Leave the required amount of headspace between paper and lid.

Sugar Packs: Often these are used for softer, juicier fruits. Place the prepared fruit in a large glass bowl, and sprinkle with the required amount of sugar. Allow to stand a few minutes before stirring. Pack tightly in containers, being careful not to crush fruit. Leave the required headspace.

Unsweetened Packs: Although these usually yield a product that is not of the highest quality, they are sometimes needed for special diets. Figs, currants, rhubarb, blueberries, and cranberries freeze satisfactorily without sugar. Pack fruit tightly in containers, but do not crush. Leave ½-inch headspace in all containers.

Freezing Vegetables

Most vegetables freeze quite well, but a few—salad greens, celery, green onions, cucumbers, radishes, and tomatoes (except cooked or juice)—lose their crispness and do not yield a quality product.

Prepare all vegetables carefully and wash thoroughly in cold water just before blanching.

Blanch vegetables for the length of time directed in the chart. The purpose of blanching is to stop enzyme action; this helps food retain good color, flavor, texture, and nutritive value. It also cleans and shrinks the food.

Blanching: These steps are a guide to blanching vegetables.

1) Place 1 pound of prepared vegetables in basket of blancher, wire-mesh basket, colander, or cheesecloth bag.

2) Immerse the container in 1 gallon boiling water (2 gallons for leafy vegetables). Cover and boil for the time indicated in the Blanching Chart. Start timing immediately, allowing 1 minute longer in areas over 5,000 feet above sea level.

3) Cool vegetables quickly after removing from boiling water: immerse in ice water for a few minutes or until chilled. Drain well before packaging.

Vegetables	Blanching Time In Minutes
Asparagus	2 to 4
Beans, Green (pieces)	3
Beans, Lima	2 to 4
Broccoli (spears)	3
Brussels Sprouts	3 to 5
Cauliflower (flowerets)	3
Corn (off cob)	4
Corn (on cob)	7 to 11
Greens	2 to 3
Okra (whole)	3 to 4
Peas, English	1 to 2
Peas, Black-eyed and Field	1 to 2
Squash, Summer	3
Squash, Winter	cook until tender
Tomatoes, Stewed	cook until tender

BLACKBERRIES AND DEWBERRIES

Select fully ripened berries, and handle as little as possible. Wash, cap, and drain.

Syrup Pack: Use 40% syrup. Pack berries in containers; cover with cold syrup, leaving correct headspace. Seal, label, and freeze.

Sugar Pack: Use ¾ cup sugar for each quart of berries; mix gently until sugar is dissolved. Pack in containers, leaving correct headspace. Seal, label, and freeze.

Puree: Add 1 cup sugar to each quart (2 pounds) of pureed berries, stirring until sugar is dissolved. Pack in containers, leaving correct headspace. Seal, label, and freeze.

PEACHES

Select firm, ripe peaches. Sort and wash.

Syrup Pack: Use 40% syrup; to prevent discoloration of peaches, add ascorbic-citric mixture to syrup according to label directions.

Peel peaches; halve or slice. Put directly in containers of cold syrup, leaving correct headspace. Place crumpled freezer paper on top of peaches to keep them submerged. Seal, label, and freeze.

Sugar Pack: Add ⅔ cup sugar to each quart peach halves or slices; to prevent discoloration, add ascorbic-citric mixture according to label directions. Stir gently until sugar is dissolved. Pack in containers, leaving correct headspace. Seal, label, and freeze.

Puree: Add 1 cup sugar to each quart of pureed fruit; to prevent discoloration, add ascorbic-citric mixture according to label directions. Stir until sugar is dissolved. Pack in containers, leaving correct headspace. Seal, label, and freeze.

PEARS

Peel pears; cut in halves or quarters, and remove cores. Heat pears in boiling 40% syrup for 1 to 2 minutes, depending on size of pieces. Drain and cool, reserving syrup. Chill syrup.

To prevent discoloration of pears, add ascorbic-citric mixture to cold syrup according to label directions. Pack pears in containers; cover with syrup, leaving correct headspace. Seal, label, and freeze.

LIMA BEANS

Select young, tender beans with well-filled pods. Shell and wash beans; then sort according to size. Blanch as follows: small beans, 2 minutes; medium, 3 minutes; large, 4 minutes. Cool and drain. Pack in containers, leaving ½-inch headspace. Seal, label, and freeze.

SNAP, GREEN, OR WAX BEANS

Select only fresh, tender, young pods. Wash beans, and cut off tips; then cut in lengthwise strips or in 1- or 2-inch lengths. Blanch 3 minutes. Cool and drain. Pack in containers, leaving ½-inch headspace. Seal, label, and freeze.

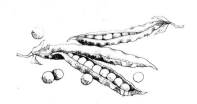

CORN

Select ears with plump, tender kernels in the milk stage (if the milk is thick and starchy, it is better to freeze the corn cream-style). Husk corn and remove silks; trim and wash.

On the Cob: Sort ears according to size. Blanch as follows: small ears, 7 minutes; medium ears, 9 minutes; large ears, 11 minutes.

Cool and drain. Package; seal, label, and freeze.

Whole Kernel: Blanch ears 4 minutes; cool and drain. Cut kernels from cob about two-thirds the depth of the kernels. Pack in containers, leaving ½-inch headspace. Seal, label, and freeze.

Cream-style: Blanch ears 4 minutes; cool and drain. Cut off tips of kernels. Scrape cobs with back of knife to remove juice and heart of kernel. Pack in containers, leaving ½-inch headspace. Seal, label, and freeze.

OKRA

Select young, tender, green pods. Wash thoroughly, and sort according to size. Remove stems at end of seed cells. Blanch as follows: small pods, 3 minutes; large, 4 minutes. Cool and drain. Leave pods whole, or slice crosswise. Pack in containers, leaving ½-inch headspace. Seal, label, and freeze.

ENGLISH OR GARDEN PEAS

Select young, tender peas. Shell and wash peas. Blanch 2 minutes. Cool and drain. Pack in containers, leaving ½-inch headspace. Seal, label, and freeze.

SUMMER SQUASH

Select young squash with small seeds and tender rind. Wash and cut into ½-inch slices. Blanch 3 minutes; cool and drain. Pack in containers, leaving ½-inch headspace. Seal, label, and freeze.

Make the most of your tomato crop with Spicy Tomato Relish (page 9), Picante Sauce (page 8), Homemade Barbecue Sauce (page 8), and Tomato Juice Cocktail (page 17).

Overleaf: *Banana Crush (page 17) can be made ahead and stored in the freezer. Spoon it into chilled glasses when you're ready to serve.*

Ways to Serve Choose plump, juicy tomatoes that are not too ripe. Wash and chill if desired. For salads slice in wedges or dice; a number of seasonings enhance the flavor. Basil leaves, chives, dill weed, oregano leaves, garlic, onion, tarragon, and Parmesan cheese.

Beverages, Sandwiches, and Snacks

Whether served as the prelude to a meal or during the meal itself, beverages, sandwiches, and snacks are always crowd-pleasers. As an added bonus, most are quick and easy to prepare and serve.

Beverages range from mealtime thirst quenchers to party fare, icy to piping hot. Sandwiches can be a complete meal or a hearty snack, and flavors are mild to spicy. Snacks are great to nibble on anytime; don't wait to have a party to try them.

CITRUS PARTY PUNCH

1½ cups crushed pineapple
2 cups orange juice
1½ cups ginger ale
2 tablespoons lemon juice
2 teaspoons cherry juice
8 maraschino cherries, halved

Spoon equal amounts of pineapple into 3 custard cups; freeze.

Combine remaining ingredients in a punch bowl; chill. Run a knife around inside edge of cups containing frozen pineapple; turn into punch. Yield: about 1 quart. *Carolyn Beyer, Fredericksburg, Tex.*

PARTY FRUIT PUNCH

2 (3-ounce) packages strawberry-flavored gelatin
1½ cups sugar
2 cups boiling water
2 (46-ounce) cans pineapple juice
2 (32-ounce) bottles apple juice
2 (6-ounce) cans frozen lemon juice
3 (1-ounce) bottles almond extract

Combine gelatin and sugar; add boiling water, stirring until mixture dissolves. Add remaining ingredients; stir. Serve over ice. Yield: 5½ quarts. *Mildred Clute, Marquez, Tex.*

HOT BUTTERED CRANBERRY PUNCH

4 cups (about 1 pound) fresh cranberries
2 cups water
⅔ cup firmly packed brown sugar
½ teaspoon ground cinnamon
¼ teaspoon ground allspice
¼ teaspoon ground cloves
⅛ teaspoon ground nutmeg
⅛ teaspoon salt
1½ cups water
2¼ cups unsweetened pineapple juice
Butter or margarine
Cinnamon sticks (optional)

Carefully sort and wash cranberries.

Bring 2 cups water to a boil in a medium saucepan; add cranberries, and cook about 5 minutes or until skins burst. Force cranberries through a food mill or sieve; strain puree.

Combine next 7 ingredients in a medium saucepan; bring to a boil. Add cranberry puree and pineapple juice; return to heat and simmer 5 minutes. Serve hot with a dot of butter and cinnamon stick, if desired. Yield: 1½ quarts.

Margaret Cotton,
Franklin, Va.

CHRISTMAS EGGNOG

6 eggs, separated
1½ cups sugar, divided
¼ teaspoon salt
1½ quarts milk
2 cups whipping cream
2 teaspoons vanilla extract
Ground nutmeg

Beat egg yolks; gradually add 1 cup sugar and salt, beating constantly. Gradually add milk and cream. Cook over hot water, stirring constantly, until mixture thickens and coats spoon. Cool. Add vanilla and chill. To serve, beat egg whites until foamy; gradually beat in remaining ½ cup sugar and fold into chilled custard. Spoon into chilled punch bowl and sprinkle with nutmeg. Yield: 4 quarts.

HOT MOCHA MIX

2 cups sugar
2 cups instant nonfat dry milk powder
2 cups non-dairy coffee creamer
1 cup cocoa
½ cup instant coffee powder

Combine all ingredients in a medium mixing bowl; stir well. Store mix in an airtight container.

For each serving, place 2 to 3 tablespoons mix in a cup. Add 1 cup boiling water and stir well. Yield: about 50 servings.

Mrs. Doug Hail,
Moody, Tex.

HOT SPICY CIDER

1 gallon apple cider
½ cup firmly packed brown sugar
½ teaspoon ground nutmeg
4 (4-inch) sticks cinnamon
20 whole cloves
1 (6-ounce) can frozen orange juice
    concentrate, undiluted
½ cup lemon juice
Stick cinnamon (optional)

Combine first 5 ingredients in a large saucepan. Bring to a boil; reduce heat and simmer for 10 minutes. Strain spices from cider. Add orange and lemon juice; stir until heated through. Serve hot with stick cinnamon, if desired. Yield: 16 to 18 servings.

Paula Sprinkle,
Troutville, Va.

SPICED TEA

1½ quarts boiling water
1 cup sugar
2 cups apple juice
3 cups pineapple juice
2 lemons, sliced
2 oranges, sliced
Ground cloves to taste
Ground cinnamon to taste
3 tea bags

Combine all ingredients in saucepan; simmer 15 minutes. Remove tea bags and serve hot in mugs. Yield: about 3 quarts. *Judy Berford,*
Gloster, La.

SUNSHINE SHAKE

2 cups orange juice, chilled
1 banana, cut into chunks
1 egg
1 tablespoon honey

Combine all ingredients in container of electric blender; blend until smooth. Serve immediately. Yield: 3¼ cups. *Judy Baker,*
Sanford, Fla.

BANANA CRUSH

3 bananas
1 (6-ounce) can frozen lemonade concentrate, thawed and undiluted
3 quarts lemon-lime carbonated beverage
1 (12-ounce) can frozen orange juice concentrate, thawed and undiluted
3 cups pineapple juice
3 cups water
2 cups sugar

Combine bananas and lemonade in container of electric blender; blend until smooth.
Combine banana mixture and remaining ingredients; mix well. Pour into plastic freezer containers; freeze until slushy. Yield: 5 quarts. *Pauline Lester,*
Saluda, S.C.

TOMATO JUICE COCKTAIL

5 quarts (about 24 large) tomatoes, unpeeled and chopped
2 tablespoons chopped onion
¼ cup chopped celery
½ small bay leaf
2 sprigs parsley
1 tablespoon sugar
1 tablespoon Worcestershire sauce
¼ cup lemon juice
1 tablespoon salt
½ teaspoon hot sauce

Combine first 7 ingredients in a large Dutch oven; cook over low heat 1 hour.
Press through food mill or sieve. Add remaining ingredients; bring to a boil. Cool. Refrigerate until thoroughly chilled. Yield: about 1½ quarts. *Dorothy Youk,*
Durham, Kans.

BARBECUED BEEF AND PORK BURGERS

1 tablespoon pickling spice
2 pounds cubed beef
2 pounds cubed pork
2 medium onions, chopped
1½ cups water
1 (24-ounce) bottle catsup
¼ cup vinegar
12 hamburger buns, split and toasted

Tie pickling spice in a cheesecloth bag. Place beef, pork, onion, water, and pickling spice in a heavy Dutch oven; bring to a boil. Reduce heat; cover and simmer 6 hours or until very tender.
Drain liquid; vigorously stir the meat with a meat fork until it is shredded. Stir in catsup and vinegar; simmer an additional 15 to 20 minutes. Serve on hamburger buns. Yield: 12 servings. *Nina Ward,*
Caldwell, Kans.

Tip: Crush leftover potato chips or pretzels, and use to top casseroles.

MEATBALL HERO SANDWICHES

1 pound ground beef
¼ cup minced onion
¼ cup water
1 teaspoon dried basil leaves
¾ teaspoon salt
Dash of pepper
2 tablespoons vegetable oil
1 large green pepper, sliced
1 (15½-ounce) jar spaghetti sauce
4 small French loaves (about 6 inches long)

Combine beef, onion, water, basil, salt, and pepper. Shape into 1-inch balls; brown in hot oil. Remove and set aside. Add green pepper to oil; sauté until lightly browned. Drain off excess oil. Add spaghetti sauce and meatballs to green pepper in skillet. Cover and simmer 15 minutes. Heat rolls and split open. Spoon meatball mixture into rolls. Yield: 4 servings.

Mrs. W. P. Chambers,
Louisville, Ky.

OPEN-FACED CHILI BURGERS

1½ pounds ground beef
½ cup chopped onion
1 (8-ounce) can tomato sauce
1 (1¼-ounce) package taco seasoning mix
6 hamburger buns, split
12 slices tomato
1 cup (4 ounces) shredded Cheddar cheese
¾ cup shredded lettuce
¼ cup chopped pimiento-stuffed olives
1 small onion, cut into rings and separated
1½ tablespoons chopped red and green chiles

Brown beef and chopped onion in a large skillet; drain. Stir in tomato sauce and taco seasoning; simmer 5 minutes.

Toast hamburger buns; spread with meat mixture. Place tomato slice on each sandwich and sprinkle with cheese; bake at 400° for 4 minutes. Top with remaining ingredients. Yield: 12 servings.

Dorothy Cox,
Snyder, Tex.

TASTY HAM BUNS

¼ cup butter or margarine, softened
2 tablespoons prepared mustard with horseradish
2 teaspoons poppy seeds
2 tablespoons finely chopped onion
4 hamburger buns, split
4 thin slices cooked ham
4 slices Swiss cheese

Combine butter, mustard, poppy seeds, and onion; mix well. Spread on both cut surfaces of each bun. Place 1 slice ham and 1 slice cheese on bottom half of each bun; top with remaining bun halves. Arrange sandwiches on a lightly greased baking sheet, and bake at 350° for 20 minutes or until thoroughly heated. Yield: 4 sandwiches.

Mrs. S. R. Griffith,
Memphis, Tenn.

HOT BROWN SANDWICHES

2 tablespoons margarine, melted
2 tablespoons all-purpose flour
1 teaspoon salt
⅛ teaspoon white pepper
1 cup milk
¼ to ½ cup (1 to 2 ounces) shredded Cheddar cheese
Sliced cooked chicken or turkey
4 slices bread, toasted
8 slices bacon, cooked
¼ cup grated Parmesan cheese

Combine margarine and flour; cook over low heat, stirring until smooth. Stir in salt and pepper. Gradually add milk, stirring constantly, until smooth and thickened. Add Cheddar cheese, stirring until melted.

Place chicken on toast and cover with sauce. Place 2 slices of bacon on each sandwich; sprinkle with Parmesan cheese.

Bake at 400° for 10 minutes or until Parmesan cheese melts. Yield: 4 servings.

Tip: It's easier to cut raw meat into thin slices if it is slightly frozen.

SAUCY CHICK-WICHES

4 slices cooked chicken
4 slices bread, toasted and buttered
8 slices tomato
4 slices process American cheese
1 (10½-ounce) can chicken gravy

Arrange chicken on toast; top with tomato slices. Broil 4 inches from heat for 3 minutes or until hot. Top with cheese and broil until melted. Heat gravy and spoon over sandwiches. Yield: 4 servings.   *Melody Fowler,*
Devine, Tex.

CHEESY TUNA SANDWICH

1 (3-ounce) package cream cheese, softened
2 tablespoons mayonnaise
2 tablespoons catsup
1 tablespoon Worcestershire sauce
¼ teaspoon salt
⅛ teaspoon pepper
5 or 6 drops of hot sauce
1 (9¼-ounce) can tuna, drained and flaked
Butter or margarine, softened
3 English muffins, split
6 slices tomato
6 slices process American cheese

Combine cream cheese, mayonnaise, catsup, Worcestershire sauce, salt, pepper, and hot sauce; mix well. Stir in tuna. Lightly butter each muffin half. Top each half with 1 slice tomato, tuna mixture, and 1 slice cheese. Place on a lightly greased baking sheet; bake at 325° for 20 minutes or until cheese melts and sandwich is heated through. Yield: 6 sandwiches.
Joanne Spence,
Charlottesville, Va.

CRISPY CHEESE BITS

1 cup butter or margarine
2 cups (8 ounces) shredded Cheddar cheese
2 cups all-purpose flour
2 cups crisp rice cereal

Combine butter and cheese in a medium saucepan; cook over medium heat, stirring constantly, until melted. Stir in flour and cereal; let cool slightly. Shape into ¾-inch balls; place on ungreased baking sheets and flatten with a fork. Bake at 350° for 15 to 20 minutes or until lightly browned. Yield: about 4½ dozen.
Frances Hagle,
Cross Hill, S.C.

CHEESE STRAWS

½ cup butter or margarine, softened
4 cups (16 ounces) shredded sharp Cheddar cheese
2 cups all-purpose flour
1 teaspoon salt
¼ teaspoon red pepper

Cream butter and cheese. Add dry ingredients, mixing well. Press dough together. Fill cylinder of a cookie press and pipe onto greased baking sheets in long strips 2 inches apart. Cut strips into 3-inch lengths with a knife, leaving pieces in place. Bake at 350° for 15 to 17 minutes or until crisp. Yield: about 5 dozen.
Margaret H. King,
Calhoun, Ga.

CHEESE WAFERS

1 cup all-purpose flour
½ teaspoon salt
¾ cup chopped pecans or walnuts
2 cups (8 ounces) shredded Cheddar cheese
½ cup butter or margarine, softened

Combine flour, salt, pecans, and cheese in a mixing bowl; add butter and mix well. Divide dough in half; shape each half into a 10-inch roll. Wrap in waxed paper; chill thoroughly.

Slice rolls into ¼-inch slices and place on greased cookie sheets. Bake at 350° for 15 minutes. Yield: about 6 dozen.

Note: Rolls can be prepared ahead of time and frozen. Soften at room temperature for 1½ hours, slice, and bake as directed.
Mamie Gardner,
Charlotte, N.C.

CHEESE BALL

2 cups (8 ounces) shredded medium Cheddar
    cheese
2 cups (8 ounces) shredded sharp Cheddar
    cheese
3 (3-ounce) packages cream cheese, softened
1 tablespoon hot sauce
1 tablespoon Worcestershire sauce
Ground paprika
Chili powder
Chopped pecans

Combine cheese, hot sauce, and Worcestershire sauce; mix well. Shape into a ball. Combine paprika, chili powder, and pecans; roll cheese ball in mixture. Refrigerate until firm. Yield: one (1½-pound) cheese ball.

Sharon Shelley,
East Ridge, Tenn.

CHEESE LOG

2 (8-ounce) packages cream cheese, softened
1½ cups finely chopped pecans, divided
½ cup finely chopped celery
¼ cup finely chopped green pepper
2 tablespoons finely chopped onion
2 teaspoons seasoning salt

Combine cream cheese, ½ cup pecans, and remaining ingredients until thoroughly blended. Shape into two 8-inch logs. Roll in remaining pecans; chill. Yield: two 8-inch logs.

Helen Cantrell,
Little Rock, Ark.

CARAMEL CORN

2 cups firmly packed brown sugar
1 cup butter or margarine
½ cup white corn syrup
2 teaspoons salt
1 teaspoon soda
1 cup peanuts or pecans
7½ quarts popped corn

Combine first 4 ingredients in a saucepan. Bring to a boil; boil 5 minutes. Beat in soda. Stir in peanuts. Place corn in a shallow pan; pour sugar mixture over corn; stir. Bake at 200° for 1 hour, stirring every 15 minutes. Yield: 7½ quarts.

Rosemary Bowers,
Seminole, Tex.

SUNSHINE GRANOLA

3 cups regular oats, uncooked
1 (1½-ounce) package sesame seeds
1 cup sunflower seeds
1 cup wheat germ
½ cup vegetable oil
½ cup honey
1 cup golden seedless raisins
1 cup dried apricots, diced
1 cup dates, chopped
1 cup flaked coconut
1 cup sliced almonds

Combine first 4 ingredients. Stir oil and honey together; pour over dry mixture, stirring well. Spread mixture on a lightly greased cookie sheet; bake at 250° for 45 to 50 minutes. Allow mixture to cool; break into large pieces. Combine pieces with remaining ingredients. Store in an airtight container. Yield: about 12 cups.

PARTY O'S

4 cups toasted oat cereal
2 cups pretzel sticks
1 cup pecans or walnuts
¼ cup butter or margarine, melted
1 tablespoon Worcestershire sauce
1 teaspoon paprika
½ teaspoon garlic salt

Combine cereal, pretzel sticks, and pecans in an ungreased 13- x 9- x 2-inch baking pan. Combine remaining ingredients; pour over cereal mixture, tossing until well coated.

Bake at 275° for 30 minutes; stir occasionally. Store in an airtight container. Yield: 7 cups.

Margaret L. Hunter,
Princeton, Ky.

VEGETABLE DIP

1 (8-ounce) carton commercial sour cream
¼ cup minced green pepper
¼ cup minced celery
¼ cup minced onion
1 tablespoon minced pimiento-stuffed olives
1 tablespoon peeled and minced cucumber
1 tablespoon Worcestershire sauce
1 teaspoon lemon juice
4 to 5 drops of hot sauce
¼ teaspoon salt
⅛ teaspoon pepper

Combine all ingredients, mixing well; chill.
Yield: about 2 cups.   *Gayle Stewart,*
                                      Troy, Ala.

CHIPPED BEEF DIP

2 (8-ounce) packages cream cheese, softened
1 (10¾-ounce) can cream of mushroom soup,
    undiluted
¼ cup catsup
1 (2½-ounce) jar sliced dried beef, chopped
1 small onion, finely chopped

Combine all ingredients, stirring until
thoroughly mixed. Blend half of mixture at a
time in an electric blender until smooth. Yield:
about 3 cups.   *Helen B. Williams,*
                              Abilene, Tex.

HAM-STUFFED CELERY

1 (8-ounce) package cream cheese, softened
1 (2¼-ounce) can deviled ham
½ cup sandwich spread
¼ cup diced green pepper
1 tablespoon diced onion
2 tablespoons chopped pimiento
Celery stalks, cut into 3-inch pieces

Combine cream cheese and ham; mix until
smooth. Stir in remaining ingredients except
celery; mix well. Chill. Spread on celery. Yield:
about 1½ cups.   *Karen Cromer,*
                              Anderson, S.C.

PARTY PIZZAS

1 (10-ounce) can refrigerated flaky biscuits
¾ pound ground beef, cooked and drained
1 (6-ounce) can tomato paste
½ teaspoon salt
½ teaspoon garlic salt
½ teaspoon Worcestershire sauce
¼ teaspoon dried oregano leaves
¼ teaspoon dried thyme leaves
2 to 3 drops of hot sauce
2 cups (8 ounces) shredded mozzarella cheese

Arrange biscuits on ungreased baking
sheet 5 inches apart. Flatten biscuits into 4-inch
circles. Spread beef evenly over dough.

Combine tomato paste, salt, garlic salt,
Worcestershire sauce, oregano, thyme, and hot
sauce; spread mixture evenly over beef and
sprinkle with cheese. Bake at 425° for 13 minutes or until browned. Yield: 10 servings.
                              Vicki Dutton,
                              Brownwood, Tex.

CHOCOLATE NUT CRUNCH

½ cup chopped pecans
¾ cup firmly packed brown sugar
½ cup butter
1 (6-ounce) package semisweet chocolate
    morsels

Sprinkle pecans in a lightly greased 9-inch
square baking pan, leaving a 1-inch margin
from edges of pan.

Combine sugar and butter in a small saucepan; cook over low heat, stirring constantly,
until mixture reaches a boil. Boil 4 minutes,
stirring constantly. Remove from heat; pour
over pecans in pan.

Sprinkle chocolate morsels over top of butter mixture; cover with foil and let stand 2
minutes. Remove foil and spread melted morsels evenly over top. Chill at least 3 hours or
until firm. Break candy into serving pieces;
store in refrigerator. Yield: 6 to 8 servings.
                              Lois Ann Thomas,
                              Brooksville, Ky.

CHOCOLATE-COVERED PECAN FRITTERS

1 (14-ounce) package vanilla caramels
2 tablespoons evaporated milk
2 cups pecan halves
1 (8-ounce) milk chocolate bar
⅓ bar paraffin, broken into pieces

Combine caramels and milk in top of double boiler; heat until caramels melt, stirring occasionally. Beat with wooden spoon until creamy. Add pecans; stir well to combine. Drop by teaspoonfuls onto buttered waxed paper; let stand 15 minutes.

Break chocolate into squares and melt with paraffin in top of double boiler; heat until melted and smooth, stirring occasionally. Dip each fritter into chocolate with a toothpick; place on waxed paper to cool. Yield: 4 dozen.

SOUTHERN SALTED PECANS

1 cup butter
4 cups pecan halves
1 tablespoon salt

Melt butter in a skillet; add pecans and salt. Stir well to coat pecans; remove from heat. Place pecans in a 13- x 9- x 2-inch baking pan. Bake at 200° for 1 hour, stirring every 15 minutes. Drain on absorbent paper. Yield: 4 cups.

BROWN SUGAR PECANS

2 egg whites
¾ cup firmly packed brown sugar
1 tablespoon vanilla extract
Pinch of salt
2 cups pecan halves

Beat egg whites until stiff peaks form. Add sugar, 1 tablespoon at a time, beating well. Fold in remaining ingredients.

Drop meringue by rounded teaspoonfuls onto greased cookie sheets. Bake at 250° for 30 minutes. Remove from sheet to wire racks to cool. Yield: 6 to 7 dozen.
Reba Walley,
Purvis, Miss.

GLAZED PECANS

½ cup half-and-half
¼ cup water
1 cup sugar
1 teaspoon vanilla extract
4 cups pecan halves

Combine all ingredients except pecans in a medium saucepan; stir well. Place over medium heat, stirring constantly, until sugar dissolves; continue cooking to about 220° on candy thermometer. Remove from heat; add pecans, stirring until well coated.

Spread pecans on waxed paper, and separate with a fork. Cool. Yield: 4 cups.
Mrs. Stan Unruh,
Sedan, N. Mex.

PEANUT BRITTLE

3 cups sugar
1 cup light corn syrup
½ cup water
3 cups raw peanuts
1 tablespoon butter
1 tablespoon soda
1 teaspoon salt

Combine sugar, corn syrup, and water in a Dutch oven; cook over low heat until mixture spins a thread (230° to 234°). Add peanuts; cook to soft crack stage (about 290°), stirring constantly. Remove from heat. Add butter, soda, and salt; mix well.

Pour mixture onto 2 warm, buttered 15- x 10- x 1-inch jellyroll pans, spreading thinly. Cool and break into pieces. Yield: about 2 pounds.
Mrs. James Hardin,
Walters, Okla.

Savor the flavor of Open-Faced Chili Burgers (page 18) on a wintry day.

Overleaf: The addition of homemade Oatmeal Muffins (page 25) and Pumpkin-Nut Bread (page 27) will make any meal special.

Breads

Generations of bread baking have proven that a meal is not complete without homemade bread. Since the first colonial homemaker mixed cornmeal and water, cornbread has been a "must" with vegetables, and biscuits are a treat with any meal.

You won't soon forget the aroma of freshly baked yeast bread. Whether it's hot rolls for dinner or finger-licking honey buns for no reason at all, the breads within these pages will keep your family asking for more.

MARVELOUS APPLE MUFFINS

2 cups sifted all-purpose flour
2 tablespoons sugar
1 tablespoon baking powder
½ teaspoon salt
1 cup milk
1 egg, beaten
¼ cup butter or margarine, melted
½ cup peeled, chopped apple
¼ cup sugar
½ teaspoon ground cinnamon

Combine first 4 ingredients in a small mixing bowl; make a well in center of mixture. Combine milk, egg, and butter; add to flour mixture, stirring just until moistened.

Fill greased muffin tins two-thirds full. Top with chopped apple. Combine ¼ cup sugar and cinnamon; sprinkle 1 teaspoon sugar mixture over each muffin. Bake at 425° for 25 minutes or until lightly browned. Yield: 12 muffins.

Judy Baker,
Sanford, Fla.

OATMEAL MUFFINS

1 cup regular oats, uncooked
1 cup buttermilk
½ cup firmly packed brown sugar
½ cup vegetable oil
1 egg, beaten
1 cup all-purpose flour
1 teaspoon baking powder
½ teaspoon soda
½ teaspoon salt

Combine oats and buttermilk in medium mixing bowl; let stand for 1 hour. Add sugar, oil, and egg to oat mixture; mix well. Combine flour, baking powder, soda, and salt in a large bowl; make a well in center of mixture. Add oat mixture to dry ingredients, stirring just until moistened.

Spoon into greased muffin pans, filling two-thirds full. Bake at 400° for 20 to 25 minutes or until lightly browned. Yield: 12 muffins.

Mrs. Richard Herrington,
Hermitage, Tenn.

RAISIN-BRAN MUFFINS

1¼ cups all-purpose flour
½ cup sugar
1 tablespoon baking powder
½ teaspoon salt
2½ cups wheat bran flakes cereal
1¼ cups milk
1 egg
⅓ cup vegetable oil
¾ cup raisins

Combine flour, sugar, baking powder, and salt in a small bowl; set aside.

Combine cereal and milk in a large mixing bowl; let stand 5 minutes. Add egg and oil, beating well. Add dry ingredients and raisins, stirring just until moistened. Fill greased muffin tins two-thirds full. Bake at 400° for 30 minutes or until golden brown. Yield: about 15 muffins.

Judy Baker,
Sanford, Fla.

MEXICAN CORNBREAD

1½ cups cornmeal
1 cup canned cream-style corn
1 cup buttermilk
½ cup vegetable oil
2 eggs, beaten
1 tablespoon baking powder
1 teaspoon salt
1 teaspoon sugar
2 jalapeño peppers, seeded and minced
¼ cup finely chopped onion
2 tablespoons minced green pepper
1 cup (4 ounces) shredded sharp Cheddar
   cheese

Combine all ingredients except cheese in a large bowl; stir well. Pour half of mixture into a greased 10-inch iron skillet; top with cheese. Add remaining mixture. Bake at 450° about 30 minutes or until done. Yield: 10 to 12 servings.

Marie Johnson,
Hamburg, Ark.

MILE-HIGH BISCUITS

3 cups all-purpose flour
¼ cup sugar
1 tablespoon plus 1 teaspoon baking powder
½ teaspoon cream of tartar
¾ teaspoon salt
½ cup shortening
1 egg, beaten
1 cup plus 2 tablespoons milk

Combine dry ingredients in a mixing bowl. Cut in shortening until mixture resembles coarse crumbs. Add egg and milk all at once; mix until dough forms a ball. Turn dough out on a lightly floured surface and knead 10 to 12 times. Roll out to ¾-inch thickness; cut with floured 2½-inch biscuit cutter. Place on ungreased baking sheet and freeze. When biscuits have frozen, they may be stored in a plastic bag in the freezer until needed.

To bake frozen biscuits, place on lightly greased baking sheet; bake at 475° for 12 to 15 minutes or until light brown. Yield: 1 dozen.

Mrs. W. P. Chambers,
Louisville, Ky.

FRY BREAD

2 eggs, beaten
1 cup milk
4 cups all-purpose flour
2 teaspoons baking powder
¾ teaspoon salt
Vegetable oil

Combine eggs and milk in a medium bowl. Stir in flour, baking powder, and salt; mix well. Turn dough out on a floured surface and roll very thin. Cut into 3-inch squares. Fry in deep oil heated to 375°. Cook until brown; drain on paper towels. Serve warm with butter and honey. Yield: 2 to 2½ dozen.

Frieda Ralstin,
Wellston, Okla.

Tip: Use baking soda on a damp cloth to shine up your kitchen appliances.

APPLESAUCE-NUT BREAD

2 cups all-purpose flour
¾ cup sugar
1 tablespoon baking powder
½ teaspoon soda
1 teaspoon salt
½ teaspoon ground cinnamon
1 cup coarsely chopped walnuts
1 egg
1 cup applesauce
2 tablespoons vegetable oil

Combine flour, sugar, baking powder, soda, salt, and cinnamon; mix well. Add walnuts; stir.

Beat egg; add applesauce and oil, mixing well. Make a well in dry ingredients. Add applesauce mixture, stirring until blended. Spoon batter into a greased and floured 8½- x 4½- x 3-inch loafpan. Bake at 350° for 50 to 55 minutes or until done. Yield: 1 loaf.

Mrs. Charles Judy,
Daleville, Va.

GOLDEN HARVEST BREAD

2¼ cups all-purpose flour
4 teaspoons baking powder
1 teaspoon salt
1 cup firmly packed brown sugar
½ cup unprocessed bran
½ cup chopped walnuts
1 cup milk
1 egg
¼ cup melted butter
½ cup golden raisins

Combine first 6 ingredients; mix well. Combine milk, egg, and butter, stirring to blend. Make a well in center of dry ingredients; add egg mixture, stirring only until dry ingredients are moistened. Stir in raisins.

Pour batter into a greased and floured 9- x 5- x 3-inch loafpan. Bake at 375° for 50 to 55 minutes. Remove from pan; cool on a wire rack. Yield: 1 loaf. *Betty Freeman,*
Wilmington, N.C.

ORANGE TEA BREAD

2 cups all-purpose flour
½ cup sugar
1 teaspoon salt
1 teaspoon soda
1 egg, beaten
¼ cup butter or margarine, melted
1 teaspoon grated orange rind
1 teaspoon grated lemon rind
1 cup orange juice
1 cup chopped pecans

Combine flour, sugar, salt, and soda; add remaining ingredients, mixing well. Pour into a greased 9- x 5- x 3-inch loafpan. Bake at 350° for 50 minutes. Yield: 1 loaf.

PUMPKIN-NUT BREAD

3⅓ cups all-purpose flour
½ teaspoon baking powder
2 teaspoons soda
1½ teaspoons salt
1 teaspoon ground cinnamon
1 teaspoon ground cloves
⅔ cup shortening
2⅔ cups sugar
4 eggs
1 (16-ounce) can pumpkin
⅔ cup water
⅔ cup raisins
⅔ cup chopped pecans

Combine first 6 ingredients; set aside.

Cream shortening in a large mixing bowl; gradually add sugar, beating until light and fluffy and sugar is dissolved. Add eggs, one at a time, beating well after each addition. Add pumpkin; mix well.

Add dry ingredients alternately with water to the creamed mixture; mix well. Stir in raisins and pecans.

Spoon into 2 greased and floured 9- x 5- x 3-inch loafpans. Bake at 300° for 1½ hours. Yield: 2 loaves. *Vickie L. Carter,*
Stuart, Va.

WALNUT BREAD

½ cup butter or margarine, softened
2 cups sugar
6 eggs
1 (12-ounce) package vanilla wafers, crushed
½ cup milk
1 teaspoon vanilla extract
¼ teaspoon salt
1 cup chopped walnuts
1 tablespoon all-purpose flour
1 (3½-ounce) can flaked coconut

Cream butter; gradually add sugar, beating until light and fluffy. Add eggs, two at a time, beating well after each addition.

Add vanilla wafer crumbs alternately with milk to creamed mixture, mixing well. Add vanilla and salt; mix well.

Dredge walnuts in flour. Stir walnuts and coconut into batter. Pour batter into a greased and floured 10-inch tube pan. Bake at 350° for 1 hour and 10 minutes or until done. Yield: one 10-inch cake.   *Louise Duckett,*
Waynesville, N.C.

SOUR CREAM COFFEE CAKE

1 cup butter or margarine, softened
1¾ cups sugar, divided
3 eggs, separated
1 (8-ounce) carton commercial sour cream
2½ cups sifted all-purpose flour
1 teaspoon baking powder
1 teaspoon soda
½ teaspoon ground cinnamon
½ cup chopped nuts

Combine butter and 1½ cups sugar in a large mixing bowl, creaming until light and fluffy; add egg yolks and beat until combined. Stir in sour cream.

Combine flour, baking powder, and soda in a small bowl; add to creamed mixture, stirring until combined.

Beat egg whites until stiff; fold into batter. Pour mixture into a greased and floured 13- x 9- x 2-inch baking pan. Combine remaining ¼ cup

sugar, cinnamon, and nuts, and sprinkle over the batter.

Bake at 350° for 35 minutes or until cake tests done. Let cool 10 minutes; cut into 15 squares. Yield: one coffee cake.   *Judy Baker,*
Sanford, Fla.

LAYERED SOUR CREAM COFFEE CAKE

1 cup butter or margarine, softened
2 cups sugar
3 eggs
2 cups all-purpose flour
¼ teaspoon salt
1 teaspoon baking powder
1 (8-ounce) carton commercial sour cream
1 teaspoon vanilla extract
2 tablespoons sugar
1 tablespoon ground cinnamon
½ cup finely chopped pecans or walnuts

Combine butter and 2 cups sugar in a large mixing bowl; cream until light and fluffy. Add eggs, one at a time, beating well after each addition. Combine dry ingredients; add to creamed mixture alternately with sour cream, mixing slightly after each addition. Stir in the vanilla.

Combine 2 tablespoons sugar, cinnamon, and pecans. Spoon one-third of batter into a greased and floured 10-inch Bundt pan. Sprinkle with half of cinnamon mixture. Repeat layers with remaining batter and cinnamon mixture, ending with batter. Bake at 300° for 15 minutes; increase oven temperature to 325° and bake an additional 55 to 60 minutes or until cake tests done. Yield: one 10-inch coffee cake.
Sandy English,
Blakely, Ga.

CHOICE LEMON ROLLS

1 cup butter or margarine, softened and
    divided
3 cups sugar, divided
Grated rind and juice of 3 lemons
2⅓ cups self-rising flour
¼ cup plus 2 tablespoons vegetable oil
⅔ cup milk
2 cups boiling water

Combine ½ cup butter, 1½ cups sugar, and lemon rind; mix until well blended; set aside. Combine flour, oil, and milk; stir until well blended. Roll dough to ¼-inch thickness on a floured surface. Spread butter mixture evenly over dough. Roll up jellyroll fashion; cut into ¾-inch-thick slices. Place slices cut side down in a lightly greased 13- x 9- x 2-inch pan. Bake at 400° about 25 minutes or until golden brown.

Combine boiling water, remaining ½ cup butter, remaining 1½ cups sugar, and lemon juice; heat to boiling. Pour sauce over hot slices. Serve warm. Yield: about 16 servings.

Helen Kelley,
Eldridge, Ala.

HONEY-OATMEAL BUNS

¼ cup sugar
2 packages dry yeast
2 teaspoons salt
1 cup regular oats, uncooked
4½ to 5 cups all-purpose flour, divided
½ cup water
1 cup milk
¼ cup butter or margarine
2 eggs
Honey Topping
⅔ cup chopped pecans
¼ cup butter or margarine, melted
½ cup firmly packed brown sugar
2 teaspoons ground cinnamon

Combine sugar, yeast, salt, oats, and 1½ cups flour in large bowl. Set aside.

Heat water, milk, and ¼ cup butter in a small saucepan to 120° to 130°. Add to dry ingredients; beat 2 minutes at medium speed of electric mixer, scraping bowl occasionally. Add 1 cup flour and eggs; beat 2 minutes at high speed. Stir in enough remaining flour to make a soft dough.

Turn dough out onto a lightly floured surface and knead until smooth and elastic, about 8 to 10 minutes. Place in a greased bowl, turning to grease top. Cover; let rise in a warm place (85°), free from drafts, 1 hour or until doubled in bulk. Punch dough down, and let rest 10 minutes.

Prepare Honey Topping; pour into two lightly greased 9-inch square non-stick pans. Tilt pans to cover evenly. Sprinkle half of pecans in each pan. Set aside.

Divide dough in half. Roll one half into a 12- x 9-inch rectangle on a lightly floured board. Brush with half of melted butter. Combine brown sugar and cinnamon; stir. Sprinkle half of cinnamon mixture on each rectangle, leaving a ½-inch margin on all sides. Roll up each rectangle, starting at long end, jellyroll fashion. Pinch edge and ends to seal. Cut each roll into twelve 1-inch slices. Arrange cut side down in prepared pans. Cover and let rise until doubled in bulk.

Bake at 375° for 25 minutes. Cool 5 minutes on a rack; invert onto plate. Yield: 2 dozen.

HONEY TOPPING:

½ cup honey
½ cup firmly packed brown sugar
¼ cup butter or margarine
¼ teaspoon salt

Combine honey, sugar, butter, and salt in a small saucepan; bring to a boil, stirring constantly. Simmer for 1½ to 2 minutes. Yield: about 1 cup.

Dorothy L. Anderson,
Manor, Tex.

Tip: To freshen dry rolls or French bread sprinkle with a few drops of water, wrap in aluminum foil, and reheat at 350° about 10 minutes.

ALMOND SWIRL RING

1 cup milk
¼ cup plus 2 tablespoons butter or margarine
⅓ cup sugar
½ teaspoon salt
3½ to 4 cups all-purpose flour, divided
1 package dry yeast
1 egg, beaten
⅓ cup sugar
2 tablespoons butter or margarine, softened
½ cup ground almonds
¼ teaspoon almond extract
1½ cups sifted powdered sugar
2 to 3 tablespoons milk or water
Candied cherry halves
Whole blanched almonds, toasted

Combine milk, ¼ cup plus 2 tablespoons butter, ⅓ cup sugar, and salt in a small saucepan; stir over low heat until butter melts. Cool to lukewarm (about 115°). Combine 2 cups flour and yeast in a large bowl; add warm milk mixture and egg. Beat well. Add enough remaining flour to make a soft dough.

Turn dough out on a floured surface, and knead 3 to 5 minutes; shape into a ball. Place in a greased bowl, turning to grease top. Cover; let rise in a warm place (85°), free from drafts, until doubled in bulk (about 1 hour). Punch dough down, and let rise 10 additional minutes.

Place dough on a floured surface, and roll into an 18- x 12-inch rectangle. Combine ⅓ cup sugar, 2 tablespoons butter, ground almonds, and almond extract; blend well, and sprinkle over dough, leaving ½-inch margin on all sides. Starting with long edge, roll dough up jellyroll fashion; pinch edges together to seal.

Place roll on a greased cookie sheet; shape into a ring, and pinch ends together to seal. Using kitchen shears or a sharp knife, make a cut every inch around ring (cut should go two-thirds of way through roll). Gently pull slices out and twist, overlapping slices slightly. Cover; let rise in a warm place (85°), free from drafts, until doubled in bulk (about 45 minutes).

Bake at 375° for 15 to 20 minutes or until golden brown. Combine powdered sugar and 2 to 3 tablespoons milk to make a glaze; drizzle over hot ring. Garnish with candied cherries and almonds. Yield: 16 to 20 servings.

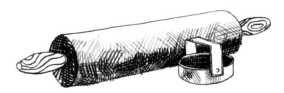

OLD-FASHIONED SPICY DOUGHNUTS

1 package dry yeast
¼ cup warm water (105° to 115°)
1 cup milk
¼ cup shortening
½ teaspoon salt
5 cups all-purpose flour, divided
1½ teaspoons ground cinnamon
¼ teaspoon ground nutmeg
⅛ teaspoon ground mace
¾ cup sugar
3 eggs, beaten
Vegetable oil
2½ cups powdered sugar
6 tablespoons plus 2 teaspoons water

Dissolve yeast in warm water. Scald milk; stir in shortening and salt. Cool to lukewarm; stir in yeast and 2½ cups flour. Combine spices and sugar; add spice mixture and eggs to flour mixture. Stir in remaining 2½ cups flour.

Turn out on a lightly floured board and knead until smooth and elastic. Place in a greased bowl, turning to grease top. Cover and let rise in a warm place (85°), free from drafts, about 1½ hours or until doubled in bulk.

Punch dough down; place on a lightly floured board, and roll to ½-inch thickness. Cut with a floured doughnut cutter; cover doughnuts and let rise in a warm place, free from drafts, about 1½ hours or until doubled in bulk.

Fry in hot oil (375°), turning until golden brown. Drain on paper towels. Combine powdered sugar and water; coat warm doughnuts in sugar glaze; place on waxed paper. Yield: about 2½ dozen.

Mrs. W. R. Wimberly,
Yoakum, Tex.

ANGEL BISCUITS

1 package dry yeast
¼ cup warm water (105° to 115°)
2½ cups self-rising flour
1 teaspoon baking powder
1 teaspoon salt
2 tablespoons sugar
½ cup shortening
1 cup buttermilk

Dissolve yeast in warm water; set aside. Combine dry ingredients in a mixing bowl; cut in shortening until mixture resembles coarse crumbs. Add buttermilk, mixing well. Add yeast mixture; mix until dough forms a ball. Cover and chill overnight.

Turn dough out on a lightly floured surface and roll to ½-inch thickness; cut with a 2½-inch biscuit cutter. Place on lightly greased cookie sheet and bake at 400° for 10 to 12 minutes or until light brown. Yield: about 1½ dozen.

Mrs. Doug Hail,
Moody, Tex.

OAT-MOLASSES BREAD

2 packages dry yeast
½ cup warm water (105° to 115°)
1⅓ cups warm milk
1 cup hot water
¼ cup shortening
⅓ cup molasses
4 teaspoons salt
7 to 7¾ cups all-purpose flour, divided
2½ cups regular oats, uncooked
2 tablespoons melted butter
1 tablespoon milk

Combine yeast and ½ cup warm water in a small bowl; let stand 5 minutes.

Combine 1⅓ cups milk, 1 cup water, and shortening in a large bowl; stir until shortening is melted. Stir in molasses, salt, and the yeast mixture.

Gradually add 2 cups flour, beating well. Add oats and enough remaining flour to form a stiff dough.

Turn out dough onto a floured surface, and knead until smooth and elastic (about 10 minutes). Divide dough in half, and place each half in a well-greased bowl. Brush tops with butter. Cover with plastic wrap. Let rise in a warm place (85°), free from drafts, 1 hour or until doubled in bulk. Punch dough down, and let rest 10 minutes.

Shape each half into a loaf, and place each loaf in a greased 9- x 5- x 3-inch loafpan. Brush tops lightly with milk.

Cover; let rise in a warm place, free from drafts, 45 minutes. Bake at 350° for 40 to 45 minutes. Yield: 2 loaves.

Mrs. Tissie M. Brown,
Livingston, Tenn.

WHOLE WHEAT HONEY BREAD

1 package dry yeast
½ cup warm water (105° to 115°)
½ cup scalded milk
2 tablespoons honey
2 tablespoons butter or margarine
1½ teaspoons salt
1 cup whole wheat flour
2 to 2½ cups all-purpose flour

Combine yeast and water; let stand 5 minutes. Combine milk, honey, butter, and salt in a large bowl; stir until the butter is melted. Cool to lukewarm.

Stir yeast mixture and whole wheat flour into milk mixture. Gradually add enough all-purpose flour to form a stiff dough, beating well after each addition.

Turn dough out onto a lightly floured surface and knead until smooth and elastic. Shape into a ball. Place dough in a greased bowl and turn to grease top. Cover and let stand in a warm place (85°), free from draft, for 1 to 1½ hours or until doubled in bulk.

Punch dough down. Shape into a loaf and place in a lightly greased 9- x 5- x 3-inch loafpan. Cover loaf and let rise 45 minutes or until doubled in bulk. Bake at 375° for 30 minutes or until done. Yield: 1 loaf.   *Nina Ward,*
Caldwell, Kans.

NEVER-FAIL PAN ROLLS

¾ cup sugar
¾ cup shortening
1 cup boiling water
2 packages dry yeast
1 cup warm water (105° to 115°)
2 eggs, slightly beaten
6 to 7 cups all-purpose flour, divided
1 teaspoon salt
1 teaspoon baking powder
½ teaspoon soda

Cream sugar and shortening until light and fluffy. Add boiling water, mixing thoroughly; set aside to cool.

Dissolve yeast in 1 cup warm water; set aside. Add eggs to cooled shortening mixture, mixing well; stir in yeast mixture. Combine 5 cups flour with salt, baking powder, and soda; add to yeast mixture, and mix well. Turn out dough on a well-floured surface; knead in enough remaining flour until dough is no longer sticky.

Roll dough into 1½-inch balls with the hands, and place in 2 greased 9-inch round cakepans. Cover and let rise in warm place until doubled in bulk (about 1½ hours). Bake at 400° for 20 minutes or until golden brown. Yield: about 3 dozen.

Note: Dough may be stored in refrigerator until ready to use; brush surface with vegetable oil, and place in a covered container.

Mrs. Robert W. McNeil,
Ronceverte, W. Va.

FRENCH-FRIED ROLLS

¼ cup shortening
¼ cup sugar
1 teaspoon salt
½ cup boiling water
1½ cups evaporated milk
1 package dry yeast
1 egg, beaten
4 to 4½ cups all-purpose flour
Vegetable oil

Combine shortening, sugar, salt, and water in a large bowl; stir occasionally to melt shortening and dissolve sugar. Add milk, and allow mixture to cool to 105° to 115°. Dissolve yeast in liquid mixture; let stand 5 minutes. Stir egg into yeast mixture; gradually stir in flour to form a soft dough.

Turn dough out onto a floured surface, and knead lightly until smooth (3 to 5 minutes). Cover dough and let rest 5 minutes.

Heat 1½ inches of oil to 350°. Drop dough by tablespoonfuls into oil; cook 4 to 5 minutes on each side or until golden brown. Drain on paper towels. Serve hot. Yield: 3 dozen.

Mrs. Kenneth A. Brewer,
Lafayette, La.

CORNBREAD DRESSING

6 to 8 cups stale bread, torn into bite-size pieces
2 cups crumbled cornbread
1 (8-ounce) package herb-seasoned stuffing mix
3½ cups chicken or turkey broth
½ cup hot water
1 cup chopped onion
½ cup butter or margarine, melted
1 tablespoon salt
Pepper to taste
½ teaspoon ground sage

Combine first 7 ingredients; sprinkle with salt, pepper, and sage, and mix well. Spoon dressing into a greased 13- x 9- x 2-inch baking dish and bake at 325° for 45 minutes. Yield: about 12 servings.

Jean Moore,
Staunton, Va.

Enjoy the old-fashioned flavor of molasses with these favorites: (front to back) Butter Pecan Cookies (page 81), Oat-Molasses Bread (page 31), and Molasses Sugar Cookies (page 79).

Overleaf: Leftover ham flavored with mushrooms, cheese, and onions makes hearty Ham and Macaroni Casserole (page 41).

Main Dishes

Main dishes are the backbone of any meal, be it breakfast, lunch, or dinner. And whether it's pot roast for Sunday dinner or country ham to start off those cold winter mornings, you can be sure meat is a favorite of all.

And it's not unusual for wild game to grace the Southern dinner table. The South is a hunter's paradise—quail, dove, duck, and venison are limited only by the hunting season, or by the "ones that got away."

LASAGNA

1 pound ground beef
2 tablespoons hot vegetable oil
1 (28-ounce) can whole tomatoes, undrained and coarsely chopped
2 (6-ounce) cans tomato paste
2 teaspoons salt
1 teaspoon Italian seasoning
¼ teaspoon pepper
¼ teaspoon crushed red pepper
⅛ teaspoon garlic powder
1 (8-ounce) package lasagna noodles
1 cup (4 ounces) shredded mozzarella cheese
1 cup ricotta or small curd cottage cheese
¼ cup grated Parmesan cheese
4 slices mozzarella cheese, cut diagonally

Brown ground beef in oil in a large skillet, stirring to crumble; drain off pan drippings. Stir tomatoes, tomato paste, and seasonings into meat. Bring to a boil; reduce heat and simmer 40 minutes, stirring occasionally.

Cook noodles according to package directions; drain.

Place half of lasagna noodles in a lightly greased 12- x 8- x 2-inch baking dish, slightly overlapping lengthwise edges. Spoon one-third of meat mixture over noodles; add half of shredded mozzarella cheese, cottage cheese, and Parmesan cheese. Repeat layers, and spoon on remaining meat mixture. Arrange mozzarella slices on top. Bake at 350° for 30 minutes or until cheese is melted. Yield: 6 to 8 servings.

Lou Harper,
Edmonton, Ky.

LAYERED GRECIAN BAKE

1½ pounds ground beef
½ cup chopped onion
½ cup dry breadcrumbs
1 egg, slightly beaten
1¼ teaspoons salt
1 teaspoon basil leaves
¼ teaspoon pepper
2 (8-ounce) cans tomato sauce with cheese
1 small eggplant, peeled and cut into ½-inch slices
1 cup (4 ounces) shredded Cheddar cheese
½ cup commercial sour cream

Combine first 7 ingredients; stir in 1 can tomato sauce. Divide meat mixture in half; spread one half in an 8-inch square baking dish. Place eggplant slices on top of meat mixture. Combine cheese and sour cream; spread over eggplant. Top with remaining meat mixture and spread evenly. Bake at 350° for 1 hour; drain and discard excess fat. Pour 1 can tomato sauce over meat. Bake 15 minutes longer. Yield: 6 servings.
Mrs. Bill Guthrie,
Mt. Sterling, Ky.

SOUR CREAM ENCHILADA CASSEROLE

1 cup water
2 tablespoons picante sauce
12 corn tortillas
2 pounds ground beef
1 onion, chopped
1 to 1½ teaspoons salt
⅛ teaspoon pepper
2 teaspoons ground cumin
1 tablespoon chili powder
1 teaspoon garlic powder
¾ cup ripe olives, sliced
¼ cup picante sauce
½ cup butter or margarine
2 tablespoons all-purpose flour
1½ cups milk
1 (16-ounce) carton commercial sour cream
2 cups (8 ounces) shredded Cheddar cheese

Combine water and 2 tablespoons picante sauce in a large shallow dish. Place tortillas in picante sauce mixture; let stand 5 minutes. Drain.

Cook ground beef and onion in a heavy skillet until brown; drain off excess grease. Stir in salt, pepper, cumin, chili powder, garlic, olives, and remaining picante sauce; simmer meat mixture 5 minutes.

Melt butter in a heavy saucepan over low heat; add flour, stirring until smooth. Cook 1 minute, stirring constantly. Gradually stir in milk; cook over medium heat, stirring constantly, until thickened and bubbly. Remove from heat and add sour cream; stir until well blended.

Place half of tortillas in a 13- x 9- x 2-inch baking dish. Pour half of sour cream sauce over tortillas; spoon half of meat mixture evenly over sauce. Sprinkle half of cheese over meat mixture. Repeat layering with remaining ingredients. Bake at 375° for 25 minutes. Yield: 8 servings.
Mrs. Hubert Watson,
Caldwell, Tex.

MEAT AND CHEESE LOAF

1½ pounds ground beef
1 egg, beaten
1 cup uncooked regular oats
½ cup chopped onion
1 cup diced Cheddar cheese
1 large green pepper, finely chopped
1 teaspoon celery salt
½ teaspoon paprika
2 teaspoons salt
¼ teaspoon pepper
1 tablespoon Worcestershire sauce
1 cup milk

Combine all ingredients in a medium bowl; mix well. Pack into a lightly greased 9-inch loafpan. Bake at 350° for 1 hour and 10 minutes or until done. Yield: 6 to 8 servings.
Mrs. Lola Sumerford,
Gatesville, Tex.

STUFFED CABBAGE ROLLS

1 medium head cabbage
1¼ pounds ground beef
1 egg
1 cup minced onion
½ cup uncooked regular rice
2 tablespoons butter or margarine, melted
2 teaspoons salt
½ teaspoon pepper
½ cup grated Parmesan cheese
1 (28-ounce) can whole tomatoes

Gently remove the outer 10 leaves from cabbage; reserve remaining cabbage for use in other recipes.

Put about 1 inch of water in a large Dutch oven; bring to a boil. Add cabbage leaves; cover, reduce heat, and simmer 5 minutes. Drain cabbage leaves.

Combine ground beef, egg, onion, rice, butter, salt, and pepper; mix well. Place equal portions of meat mixture in center of cabbage leaves. Fold ends over and roll up. Place cabbage rolls, seam side down, in a large greased skillet. Sprinkle cheese over cabbage rolls.

Drain tomatoes, reserving 1 cup juice. Arrange tomatoes on top of cabbage rolls. Pour reserved tomato juice over cabbage rolls. Bring mixture to a boil over high heat; reduce heat and simmer, uncovered, for 1 hour. Yield: 10 servings.
Penny Petty,
Burlington, N.C.

FIRESIDE BLISS

1 (2-pound) boneless chuck roast
1 (1.25-ounce) package beef-flavored
   mushroom soup mix
¼ teaspoon salt
¼ teaspoon pepper
1 (14½-ounce) can whole tomatoes
6 small onions
4 carrots, cut in 1½-inch pieces
1 tablespoon cornstarch

Slice roast into serving portions. Place meat in center of a 13- x 9- x 2-inch baking dish

lined with a large sheet of heavy-duty aluminum foil; sprinkle with soup mix, salt, and pepper.

Drain and chop tomatoes, reserving ½ cup juice. Add tomatoes, onions, and carrots to meat.

Combine reserved tomato juice and cornstarch, blending well. Pour tomato juice mixture over meat and vegetables. Seal foil and bake at 350° for 2 hours. Yield: 4 to 6 servings.
Ruth Wilson,
Siler City, N.C.

SAUCY CHUCK ROAST

1½ cups catsup
1 cup sliced pimiento-stuffed olives
1 medium onion, chopped
¼ cup water
⅓ cup lemon juice
¾ cup sliced fresh mushrooms
3 tablespoons Worcestershire sauce
1 bay leaf
1 to 2 tablespoons sugar
¾ teaspoon coarsely ground pepper
⅛ teaspoon hot sauce
1 (4-pound) boneless chuck roast (about 1½
   inches thick)
3 tablespoons cornstarch
¼ cup water

Combine first 11 ingredients in a mixing bowl; mix well. Pour half of sauce in a 13- x 9- x 2-inch baking dish; place roast on top and add remaining sauce. Cover; marinate roast several hours or overnight in refrigerator; turn roast occasionally and spoon sauce over top. Cook, covered, at 350° for 2 hours or until tender. Place roast on a serving platter; keep warm.

Skim oil from sauce, and remove bay leaf. Pour sauce into a saucepan. Dissolve cornstarch in ¼ cup water, stirring until smooth. Stir cornstarch mixture into sauce. Cook over medium heat, stirring constantly, until sauce is thickened and bubbly. Slice roast and serve with sauce. Yield: 8 to 10 servings.
Bonnie McCann,
Vanceburg, Ky.

HIGHLAND POT ROAST

2 tablespoons shortening
1 (2- to 2½-pound) boneless pot roast (bottom round, chuck, or rump)
8 small new potatoes, peeled
2 stalks celery, cut into 2-inch pieces
4 medium carrots, quartered and cut into 2-inch pieces
1½ teaspoons salt
¼ teaspoon pepper
16 dried apricots
1 cup sliced fresh mushrooms
1 cup catsup

Melt shortening in a Dutch oven, and brown roast on all sides. Place roast in a 13- x 9- x 2-inch baking dish; arrange potatoes, celery, and carrots around roast. Sprinkle salt and pepper over roast and vegetables. Top meat with apricots and mushrooms. Pour catsup over all ingredients.

Cover and bake at 325° for 2 hours. Yield: 6 servings.

Betty Oakes,
Hurt, Va.

PEPPERY BRISKET ROAST

1 teaspoon garlic salt
1 teaspoon onion salt
2 teaspoons celery salt
1½ teaspoons salt
2 teaspoons Worcestershire sauce
2 teaspoons pepper
1 tablespoon liquid smoke
1 (3- to 4-pound) well-trimmed boneless beef brisket
3 tablespoons brown sugar
1 tablespoon dry mustard
Dash of ground nutmeg
1 tablespoon soy sauce
1 tablespoon lemon juice
3 drops of hot sauce
½ cup catsup

Combine first 7 ingredients, mixing well; spread brisket evenly with mixture, and place in a greased 13- x 9- x 2-inch baking dish. Cover and chill 8 to 10 hours or overnight.

Allow brisket to come to room temperature; cover and bake at 300° for 30 minutes.

Combine remaining ingredients; mix well and pour over brisket. Cover and bake 1 to 1½ hours or until done. Yield: 6 to 8 servings.

Lucille Davis,
Whitesboro, Tex.

EASY SHORTRIBS

4 pounds lean beef shortribs
2 tablespoons vegetable oil
2 medium onions, finely chopped
1 (15-ounce) can tomato sauce
1 cup water
¼ cup firmly packed brown sugar
¼ cup vinegar
½ teaspoon salt
1 teaspoon dry mustard
1 teaspoon Worcestershire sauce
Hot cooked rice or noodles

Brown ribs in oil in a large Dutch oven. Combine next 8 ingredients in a small bowl; stir until blended and pour over ribs. Cover and simmer over low heat 2 to 2½ hours. Serve over rice or noodles. Yield: 6 to 8 servings.

Mrs. E. Raymond Ward,
Brookneal, Va.

MEAT-VEGETABLE KABOBS

½ cup soy sauce
¼ cup vegetable oil
1 tablespoon dark corn syrup
2 cloves garlic, minced
1 teaspoon dry mustard
1 teaspoon ground ginger
2½ pounds boneless sirloin, cut into 1½-inch cubes
3 medium-size green peppers, cut into 1-inch squares
5 small tomatoes, quartered

Combine first 7 ingredients; mix well. Add meat; cover and chill 8 to 10 hours or overnight.

Remove meat from marinade. Alternate meat and vegetables on skewers. Grill kabobs 20 to 25 minutes over medium heat, basting with marinade and turning occasionally. Yield: 6 servings. *Mary Avery, McGehee, Ark.*

BRAISED LIVER

Vegetable oil
1 pound sliced calves liver, skinned and membrane removed
Salt and pepper to taste
1 cup finely chopped onion
1 clove garlic, finely chopped
1 cup sliced mushrooms

Heat a small amount of oil over low heat in a skillet. Sprinkle liver with salt and pepper; place in skillet. Top with onion, garlic, and mushrooms; cover and cook over low heat for 15 to 20 minutes or until tender but not brown. Yield: 4 to 6 servings. *Brenda Hamblin, Miami Lakes, Fla.*

SPINACH-EGG SCRAMBLE

1 pound fresh spinach
¼ cup chopped onion
3 tablespoons butter or margarine
¾ cup chopped cooked ham
3 eggs
½ teaspoon salt
⅛ teaspoon seasoned pepper
1 tablespoon lemon juice

Wash spinach thoroughly and drain; cook in a covered saucepan, without adding water, about 5 minutes or until tender, turning frequently. Drain well and chop.

Sauté onion in butter until tender; add ham. Beat eggs until light and lemon colored; stir in salt, pepper, and lemon juice. Add egg mixture and spinach to onion and ham; cook over medium heat. As eggs begin to set, lift cooked portion so that uncooked portion can flow to bottom. Cook until eggs are thickened but still moist (about 3 to 5 minutes). Yield: 4 servings. *Mrs. Eunice Palmer, Morris Chapel, Tenn.*

FAMILY FUN OMELETS

2 eggs
2 tablespoons water
1 tablespoon butter or margarine
Fillings (suggestions follow)
Salt
Pepper

Combine eggs and water in small mixing bowl; mix with a wire whisk or fork until thoroughly blended.

Place omelet pan or skillet with sloping sides over medium heat. Add butter; gently shake pan to coat bottom and sides. Do not let butter turn brown. Pan is ready when just hot enough to sizzle a drop of water.

Pour egg mixture into pan. It should set at the sides almost immediately. With a plastic spatula, push cooked edges toward the center. Tip and tilt pan so the uncooked portions flow underneath. Move pan back and forth over heat to keep egg mixture in motion. When all liquid is set and top is still moist and creamy, add one or any combination of fillings.

Fillings should be placed on one side of omelet. (Fill omelet on left side if you are right handed, and on right side if left handed.) Slide omelet out of pan onto warmed plate and serve immediately. Season to taste. Yield: 1 serving.

Note: Omelets can be filled with a variety of ingredients. It is best to prepare fillings before beginning omelet. While eggs are still moist and creamy on top, add one or any combination of the following:
- ¼ to ⅓ cup shredded cheese
- 1 to 2 slices bacon, cooked and crumbled
- ¼ cup cubed ham
- ¼ cup sliced fresh mushrooms
- 2 tablespoons chopped green pepper
- Fresh tomato wedges, thinly sliced

Frank Baber, Cartersville, Va.

NEVER-FAIL CHEESE SOUFFLE

¼ cup butter
¼ cup plus 2 tablespoons all-purpose flour
1 cup evaporated milk
1 cup (4 ounces) shredded Cheddar cheese
1 teaspoon salt
6 eggs, separated

Wrap greased aluminum foil collar around edge of lightly greased 2-quart soufflé dish.

Melt butter in saucepan; stir in flour until smooth. Slowly stir in milk; simmer, stirring constantly, until thickened. Add cheese and salt, mixing well. Beat egg yolks; add to cheese mixture, mixing well. Cook over low heat until cheese melts and mixture is smooth. Cool about 30 minutes. Beat egg whites until stiff but not dry; fold into cheese mixture. Pour into soufflé dish. Bake at 350° for 30 minutes. Remove collar and serve at once. Yield: 8 servings.

APPLE-CHEESE QUICHE

Pastry for two 9-inch pie shells
2 cups (8 ounces) shredded sharp Cheddar cheese
1 pound mild sausage, cooked, drained, and crumbled
2 cups peeled, sliced cooking apples
1 (4-ounce) can sliced mushrooms, drained
4 eggs
1 tablespoon all-purpose flour
1 teaspoon salt
1 cup evaporated milk
1½ tablespoons butter or margarine, melted
1 apple, peeled and sliced (optional)

Line two 9-inch quiche dishes or pieplates with pastry; trim excess pastry around edges. Prick bottom and sides of quiche shell with a fork; bake at 400° for 8 minutes. Let cool on rack.

Layer cheese, sausage, 2 cups apples, and mushrooms into pastry shells. Combine eggs, flour, salt, milk, and butter; beat well. Pour half of egg mixture into each pastry shell. Bake at 375° for 45 minutes or until set. Top with apple slices, if desired. Let stand 5 minutes before serving. Yield: two 9-inch quiches.

Nancy Leonard,
Fincastle, Va.

BAKED COUNTRY HAM

1 (15-pound) sugar-cured country ham
About 1 (16-ounce) package light brown sugar
Whole cloves
Peach halves (optional)
Parsley sprigs (optional)

Scrub ham thoroughly with a stiff brush; do not soak. Pour water to 1½-inch depth in a large roasting pan. Place ham, skin side down, in roaster; coat exposed portion generously with brown sugar. Cover and bake at 350° for 4 hours, basting with pan juices every 20 to 30 minutes.

Carefully remove ham from water; remove skin. Place ham, fat side up, on a cutting board; score fat in a diamond design, and stud with cloves.

Return ham to roaster, fat side up; coat top generously with brown sugar. Continue baking, uncovered, for 1 hour. Garnish with peach halves and parsley sprigs, if desired. Yield: about 30 servings.

Note: A larger or smaller ham may be substituted. Bake 20 minutes per pound; uncover during last hour of baking time, after fat is scored and studded with cloves.

GINGERED HAM

½ cup ginger ale
½ cup orange juice
¼ cup firmly packed brown sugar
1 tablespoon vegetable oil
1½ teaspoons wine vinegar
1 teaspoon dry mustard
¼ teaspoon ground ginger
⅛ teaspoon ground cloves
1 (1½-inch-thick) slice center cut ham

Combine all ingredients except ham; mix well. Pour over ham. Cover and marinate for 8 hours in refrigerator.

Remove ham from marinade. Grill over medium coals for 1 hour and 30 minutes to 1 hour and 45 minutes or until desired degree of doneness. Baste frequently with marinade. Yield: 8 to 10 servings. *Gayle Stewart,*
Troy, Ala.

GOLDEN HAM CASSEROLE

2 cups cubed potatoes
1 cup sliced carrots
1 cup chopped celery
2 cups cubed cooked ham
2 tablespoons chopped green pepper
2 teaspoons chopped onion
3 tablespoons melted margarine
¼ cup margarine
3 tablespoons all-purpose flour
1½ cups milk
½ cup shredded Cheddar cheese
½ teaspoon salt
⅛ teaspoon pepper
½ cup breadcrumbs

Cook potatoes, carrots, and celery in a small amount of boiling unsalted water until crisp-tender; drain and set aside.

Sauté ham, green pepper, and onion in 3 tablespoons margarine in a medium skillet until ham is golden brown. Place ham mixture and reserved cooked vegetables in a greased deep 2-quart casserole.

Melt ¼ cup margarine in a heavy saucepan over low heat; add flour, stirring until smooth. Cook 1 minute, stirring constantly. Gradually stir in milk; cook over medium heat, stirring constantly, until thickened and bubbly. Stir in cheese, salt, and pepper; cook over low heat until cheese melts and mixture is slightly thickened. Pour cheese sauce over ham and vegetables; sprinkle with breadcrumbs. Bake at 375° for 25 to 30 minutes. Yield: 4 to 6 servings.
Annie Knight,
Chesnee, S.C.

HAM AND MACARONI CASSEROLE

2 cups cooked macaroni
1 pound cooked ham, cubed
1 (4-ounce) can sliced mushrooms, drained
¼ cup sliced pimiento-stuffed olives
½ cup chopped onion
2 cups commercial sour cream
3 tablespoons prepared mustard
2 to 3 teaspoons caraway seeds
½ teaspoon Worcestershire sauce
⅛ teaspoon pepper
½ cup (2 ounces) shredded Cheddar cheese

Combine macaroni, ham, mushrooms, olives, and onion in a large bowl. Combine sour cream, mustard, caraway seeds, Worcestershire sauce, and pepper, mixing well. Add ham mixture; mix well. Spoon into a greased 2-quart casserole; top with cheese. Bake at 350° for 35 to 40 minutes. Yield: 6 servings.
Mrs. Jim Pershall,
Lincoln, Ark.

PINEAPPLE-TOPPED HAM LOAF

1 (8¼-ounce) can crushed pineapple
3 tablespoons butter or margarine, melted
½ cup firmly packed brown sugar
1 pound ground lean ham
1 cup quick-cooking oats
2 eggs, slightly beaten
½ cup milk
¼ teaspoon pepper
¼ teaspoon ground ginger

Drain pineapple, reserving ¼ cup juice.

Pour butter into a 9- x 5- x 3-inch loafpan. Sprinkle brown sugar over butter; spoon pineapple evenly over brown sugar.

Combine reserved pineapple juice, ham, oats, eggs, milk, pepper, and ginger; mix well. Lightly pack mixture into loafpan. Bake at 350° for 50 to 60 minutes. Yield: 6 to 8 servings.
Dorothy L. Anderson,
Manor, Tex.

CORN-STUFFED PORK CHOPS

1 (12-ounce) can vacuum-packed corn with
  peppers, undrained
1 cup soft bread cubes
¼ cup finely chopped onion
1 teaspoon salt
½ teaspoon ground sage
6 (1-inch-thick) pork chops, cut with pockets
2 tablespoons shortening, melted
1 cup water

Combine first 5 ingredients in a medium mixing bowl; stir well. Stuff pockets of pork chops with corn mixture, and secure with wooden picks. Brown chops on both sides in shortening. Pour water over chops; cover and simmer 1 hour or until done. Yield: 6 servings.

Mrs. Steve Edgemon,
Ten Mile, Tenn.

PORK CHOPS AND POTATO SCALLOP

1 (10¾-ounce) can cream of mushroom soup,
  undiluted
½ cup commercial sour cream
¼ cup water
½ teaspoon dried dillweed
4 cups thinly sliced potatoes
4 pork chops
Salt and pepper
Vegetable oil
Parsley (optional)

Combine mushroom soup, sour cream, water, and dillweed in a small bowl; blend well. Alternate layers of potatoes and soup mixture in a lightly greased 2-quart casserole. Cover; bake at 375° for 45 minutes.

Sprinkle pork chops with salt and pepper; brown on both sides in a small amount of oil in a medium skillet. Drain on paper towels. Place chops on top of potatoes; cover and bake an additional 30 minutes. Garnish with parsley, if desired. Yield: 4 servings. *Mrs. Rita Bufkin,*
Mansfield, La.

PORK AND NOODLES

1 (3-pound) pork shoulder
1 tablespoon all-purpose flour
1 tablespoon vegetable oil
½ cup chopped celery
½ cup chopped green pepper
1 clove garlic, minced
1 teaspoon salt
¼ teaspoon paprika
⅛ teaspoon pepper
1 onion bouillon cube
1 (16-ounce) can cut green beans
½ cup commercial sour cream
1 (8-ounce) package egg noodles, cooked
¼ cup butter or margarine
½ teaspoon caraway seeds

Trim excess fat from pork; cut pork into 2- x ½-inch strips. Sprinkle flour evenly over strips; stir to coat lightly. Cook pork in hot oil in a 10-inch skillet until browned; drain off drippings. Stir in next 7 ingredients, and cook over medium heat 3 minutes.

Drain beans, reserving liquid. Add water to bean liquid to make 1 cup. Pour bean liquid over pork mixture; cover and simmer 45 minutes. Stir in green beans and sour cream.

Drain hot noodles and combine with butter and caraway seeds. Serve pork over noodles. Yield: 4 servings. *Nell Hamm,*
Louisville, Miss.

BARBECUED PORK SHOULDER

1 (3½- to 4-pound) pork shoulder roast
1 cup catsup
½ cup firmly packed brown sugar
2 teaspoons salt
1 teaspoon pepper
1 to 2 tablespoons chili powder
6 tablespoons vinegar
2 tablespoons lemon juice
¼ cup Worcestershire sauce
2 teaspoons prepared mustard
Hamburger buns (optional)

Cover roast with water in a Dutch oven. Cover and cook for 2 to 2½ hours. Thinly slice; place in a shallow 2-quart baking dish. Combine remaining ingredients except buns; spoon evenly over sliced roast. Bake at 300° for 45 minutes. Serve on buns, if desired. Yield: 6 servings.   *Brentz Moore,*
Kenton, Tenn.

CROWN ROAST OF PORK WITH CORN STUFFING

1 (16-rib) crown roast of pork
3½ teaspoons salt
⅛ teaspoon pepper
3 cups diced celery
⅔ cup minced onion
¼ cup butter or margarine, melted
8 cups soft breadcrumbs
2 (17-ounce) cans whole kernel corn, drained
2 cups boiling water
2½ teaspoons salt
1 teaspoon ground sage
¾ teaspoon pepper
Watercress or parsley (optional)
Spiced crabapples (optional)

Sprinkle roast on all sides with 3½ teaspoons salt and ⅛ teaspoon pepper; place, bone ends up, in a shallow roasting pan. Place a folded strip of aluminum foil over exposed ends of ribs. Bake, uncovered, at 325° for 30 to 35 minutes per pound. Insert meat thermometer into thickest part of roast, making certain thermometer end does not touch fat or bone; bake until thermometer registers 170°.

Cook celery in a small amount of water, covered, 15 minutes; drain. Sauté onion in butter until tender but not brown. Combine celery, onion, and remaining ingredients except watercress and crabapples; stir well. Fill center of roast with stuffing 45 minutes before roast is done; spoon remaining stuffing into a greased 1½-quart casserole and bake with roast. To serve, garnish with watercress and crabapples, if desired. Yield: 8 servings. *Mildred Howard,*
Clinton, La.

SPICY SPARERIBS

3 pounds spareribs
Seasoned meat tenderizer
1 (8-ounce) can tomato sauce
¼ cup chopped onion
2 tablespoons brown sugar
2 tablespoons barbecue sauce
2 teaspoons chili powder
2 teaspoons vinegar
1 teaspoon salt
1 teaspoon pepper
½ teaspoon Worcestershire sauce

Cut ribs into serving-size pieces, and sprinkle both sides with meat tenderizer. Place in a 13- x 9- x 2-inch baking pan. Cover and let stand 30 minutes. Bake at 350° for 45 minutes; drain off drippings.

Combine remaining ingredients; pour sauce over ribs. Bake ribs an additional 45 minutes or until tender, turning once and basting occasionally with the sauce. Yield: 2 to 3 servings.   *Mrs. Mary H. Gilliam,*
Cartersville, Va.

ORANGE BAKED CHICKEN

4 whole chicken breasts, split and skinned
¼ cup minced onion
½ teaspoon salt
¼ teaspoon rosemary
⅛ teaspoon pepper
2 tablespoons all-purpose flour
2 cups orange juice
1 (8-ounce) package wide egg noodles

Place chicken in a 15- x 10- x 1-inch jelly-roll pan. Sprinkle with onion, salt, rosemary, and pepper. Combine flour and orange juice; mix well and pour over chicken. Bake at 350° for 1 hour and 10 minutes or until done, basting with pan juices occasionally.

Prepare noodles according to package directions; drain. Arrange chicken on top of noodles on a warm platter; pour pan juices over all. Yield: 8 servings.   *Mrs. Roy McKnight,*
Abbeville, Ala.

TOMATO-BAKED CHICKEN

1 (2½- to 3-pound) broiler-fryer, cut into
    serving-size pieces
Salt and pepper
2 tablespoons vegetable oil
½ cup chopped onion
1 clove garlic, pressed
1 (16-ounce) can whole tomatoes, undrained
    and quartered
¼ cup grated Parmesan cheese
3 tablespoons all-purpose flour
½ cup commercial sour cream

Sprinkle chicken with salt and pepper; sauté in oil until brown. Remove chicken from skillet, and set aside. Sauté onion and garlic in drippings until onion is tender. Stir in tomatoes; bring to a boil.

Place chicken in a 13- x 9- x 2-inch baking dish. Pour tomato mixture over chicken. Cover and bake at 350° for 1 hour. Remove chicken to serving platter, reserving drippings. Sprinkle chicken with cheese.

Combine flour, sour cream, and drippings in a saucepan. Cook over low heat, stirring constantly, until thickened. Spoon over chicken. Yield: 4 servings. *Gwen Granderson,*
Kingsland, Ark.

BUTTERMILK CHICKEN

1 (2½- to 3-pound) broiler-fryer, cut up
4 cups buttermilk
Salt and pepper
1½ cups self-rising flour
Vegetable oil

Rinse chicken and pat dry; place in a 13- x 9- x 2-inch pan. Pour buttermilk over chicken. Cover and refrigerate 8 hours or overnight.

Remove chicken from buttermilk; season with salt and pepper. Dredge chicken in flour.

Heat 1 inch of oil in a large skillet; place chicken in skillet. Cook, uncovered, over medium heat about 30 minutes or until golden brown; turn occasionally. Drain on paper towels. Yield: 4 to 6 servings. *Susan Morgan,*
Atlanta, Ga.

CREAMED CHICKEN OVER CONFETTI RICE SQUARES

3 cups cooked rice
1 cup (4 ounces) shredded Swiss cheese
½ cup chopped parsley
⅓ cup chopped onion
⅓ cup chopped pimiento
1 teaspoon salt
3 eggs, beaten
1½ cups milk
2 tablespoons butter or margarine
3 tablespoons all-purpose flour
2 cups milk
½ teaspoon salt
¼ teaspoon ground marjoram
3 cups cubed cooked chicken
Paprika

Combine first 8 ingredients; spoon into a buttered 8-inch baking dish. Bake at 325° for 1 hour or until a knife inserted in center comes out clean.

Melt butter in a heavy saucepan over low heat; add flour, stirring until smooth. Cook 1 minute, stirring constantly. Gradually add milk; cook over medium heat, stirring, until thickened and bubbly. Stir in salt and marjoram. Add chicken; sprinkle with paprika. Cut rice into 4-inch squares. Spoon creamed chicken over rice squares. Yield: 4 servings.
Mrs. James Barden,
Suffolk, Va.

PEANUT BUTTER-MARMALADE CHICKEN

1 teaspoon salt
¼ teaspoon pepper
⅛ teaspoon ground ginger
2 whole chicken breasts, split and skinned
⅓ cup peanut butter
⅓ cup orange marmalade
3 tablespoons orange juice
1 tablespoon lemon juice
1 cup round buttery cracker crumbs
¼ cup vegetable oil

Combine salt, pepper, and ginger; rub into chicken. Combine peanut butter, marmalade, orange juice, and lemon juice. Dip chicken in this mixture; coat well with cracker crumbs. Pour oil into a 13- x 9- x 2-inch baking dish; add chicken. Bake at 350° for 30 minutes. Turn chicken and cook 30 minutes more or until done. Yield: 4 servings. *Bonnie Baumgardner, Sylva, N.C.*

CHICKEN POT PIE

1 cup chopped onion
1 cup chopped celery
1 cup chopped carrot
⅓ cup melted butter or margarine
½ cup all-purpose flour
2 cups chicken broth
1 cup half-and-half
1 teaspoon salt
¼ teaspoon pepper
4 cups chopped cooked chicken
Basic Pastry (recipe follows)
Parsley (optional)

Sauté onion, celery, and carrot in butter for 10 minutes. Add flour to sautéed mixture, stirring well; cook 1 minute, stirring constantly. Combine broth and half-and-half. Gradually stir in broth mixture; cook over medium heat, stirring constantly, until thickened and bubbly. Stir in salt and pepper. Add chicken, stirring well.

Pour chicken mixture into a shallow 2-quart casserole. Top with pastry; cut slits to allow steam to escape. Decorate with pastry cutouts, if desired. Bake at 400° for 40 minutes or until crust is golden brown. Garnish with parsley, if desired. Yield: 6 servings.

BASIC PASTRY:

1 cup all-purpose flour
½ teaspoon salt
⅓ cup plus 1 tablespoon shortening
2 to 3 tablespoons cold water

Combine flour and salt in bowl; cut in shortening with pastry blender until mixture

resembles coarse meal. Sprinkle cold water evenly over surface; stir with a fork until all dry ingredients are moistened. Shape into a ball; chill. Roll pastry to fit casserole dish. Yield: enough pastry for 2-quart casserole.
Janet Eubanks, Paris, Ark.

CHICKEN PIE WITH SWEET POTATO CRUST

3 cups diced cooked chicken
1 cup sliced cooked carrots
6 small white onions, quartered and cooked
1 tablespoon chopped fresh parsley
3 tablespoons all-purpose flour
1 cup milk
1 cup chicken broth
Salt and pepper to taste
Sweet Potato Crust

Layer first 4 ingredients in greased 2½-quart casserole.

Combine flour and a small amount of milk in a saucepan, blending until smooth; gradually stir in remaining milk and chicken broth. Place over low heat; cook until thickened, stirring constantly. Add salt and pepper.

Pour sauce over chicken and vegetables in the casserole. Cover mixture with Sweet Potato Crust, and bake at 350° about 45 minutes. Yield: 6 to 8 servings.

SWEET POTATO CRUST:

2 cups all-purpose flour
1 teaspoon baking powder
½ teaspoon salt
⅓ cup shortening
1 cup cold mashed sweet potatoes
1 egg, well beaten

Combine flour, baking powder, and salt; cut in shortening until mixture resembles coarse meal. Add sweet potatoes and egg, blending well. Roll out dough on lightly floured surface to ¼-inch thickness. Yield: crust for one pie.
Grayce E. Ball, Honaker, Va.

QUICK CHICKEN PIE

3 cups diced cooked chicken
1 (10¾-ounce) can cream of chicken soup, undiluted
1 (10¾-ounce) can chicken broth, undiluted
½ cup cooked English peas
½ cup diced cooked carrots
Salt to taste
Dash of pepper
1 (11-ounce) package piecrust sticks

Combine chicken, soup, broth, peas, carrots, and seasonings; set aside. Prepare piecrust sticks. Roll out thin; cut into 1-inch strips. Line a 1½-quart casserole with half of the piecrust strips. Pour chicken mixture into casserole. Top with remaining half of piecrust strips. Bake at 350° for 35 minutes or until crust is browned. Yield: about 6 servings. *Patsy Roberts, Eldridge, Ala.*

CHICKEN PIE

1 (2½- to 3-pound) broiler-fryer
1 stalk celery, cut into large pieces
Salt to taste
½ cup melted margarine
1 cup all-purpose flour
1 tablespoon baking powder
¼ teaspoon salt
1 cup milk
1 (10¾-ounce) can cream of celery soup, undiluted
1¼ cups chicken broth or 1 (10¾-ounce) can chicken broth, undiluted
½ teaspoon pepper

Combine chicken, celery, salt to taste, and water to cover in a Dutch oven; cover and simmer over low heat 25 to 30 minutes or until chicken is tender. Remove chicken from Dutch oven, reserving cooking liquid.

Remove chicken from bone and dice meat; place in a lightly greased 11- x 7- x 2-inch baking dish. Drizzle melted margarine over chicken.

Combine flour, baking powder, salt, and milk; beat until smooth. Pour over chicken.

Combine celery soup, chicken broth, and pepper in a small saucepan; bring to a boil over medium heat. Pour over chicken mixture. Bake at 425° about 50 minutes or until golden brown. Yield: 6 servings. *Mrs. Faye Newsom, Madison, N.C.*

CORNISH HENS WITH GIBLET DRESSING BALLS

4 (1½-pound) Cornish hens
½ cup butter or margarine, melted
Salt and pepper
1½ cups dry cornbread crumbs
1½ cups cubed dry white bread
1½ cups cubed dry wheat bread
1 cup finely chopped celery
1 cup minced onion
2½ tablespoons chopped fresh parsley
¼ teaspoon poultry seasoning
½ teaspoon salt
⅛ teaspoon pepper

Remove giblets from hens; reserve for use in dressing. Rinse hens with cold water and pat dry. Combine butter and salt and pepper; mix well. Brush cavity of each with butter mixture. Truss hens, and place breast side up on a rack in a shallow roasting pan. Bake at 350° for 1 hour and 15 minutes, basting frequently with butter mixture.

Cover reserved giblets with water; bring to a boil. Reduce heat, and cook 30 minutes or until tender. Drain giblets, reserving 1 cup broth; chop giblets. Combine giblets, reserved broth, and remaining ingredients; mix well. Roll into 1½-inch balls. Bake at 350° for 30 minutes, during last 30 minutes baking time of hens. Place hens on a serving platter; arrange dressing around hens. Yield: 4 servings. *Mrs. J. C. Graham, Athens, Tex.*

HICKORY-SMOKED TURKEY

1 (10- to 12-pound) turkey
½ cup salt
¼ cup vegetable oil
Vegetable oil
1 cup vinegar
¼ cup black pepper
2 teaspoons finely chopped fresh parsley

Rinse turkey and pat dry. Combine salt and ¼ cup oil; rub inside cavity of turkey with one-fourth of salt mixture. Truss turkey and balance on a spit; brush outside with oil.

Prepare charcoal fire in smoker and let burn 10 to 15 minutes; add 6 to 8 blocks of hickory to fire. Place a pan of water in smoker to add moisture. Put turkey on rotisserie and close hood. (If rotisserie is not available, place turkey on grill and cover with lid.)

Combine vinegar, pepper, parsley, and remaining salt mixture. Baste turkey after 1 hour. Continue cooking for 5 to 6 hours, basting occasionally. Yield: 12 to 16 servings.

Catherine Ross,
Savannah, Tenn.

GOLDEN FRIED FISH

1 cup all-purpose flour
1 tablespoon sugar (optional)
½ teaspoon salt
1 tablespoon vegetable oil
⅔ cup cold water
1 egg white
1 to 1¼ pounds fish fillets, cut into
    serving-size portions
Vegetable oil

Combine flour, sugar, salt, 1 tablespoon oil, and water; blend well. Beat egg white until soft peaks form; fold into flour mixture.

Dip fish into batter. Fry fish until golden brown on both sides in ½ inch of oil heated to 370°. Drain on paper towels. Yield: about 4 servings.

Mrs. Jack Hampton,
Elizabethton, Tenn.

FRIED CATFISH

⅓ cup yellow cornmeal
2 tablespoons all-purpose flour
1 teaspoon salt
¼ teaspoon paprika
1 pound whole catfish, cleaned and dressed
¼ cup hot vegetable oil

Combine cornmeal, flour, salt, and paprika. Dry fish thoroughly; coat both sides of fish with cornmeal mixture.

Fry fish in oil over low heat, about 4 minutes on each side or until golden brown. Drain on paper towels. Yield: 2 servings.

Note: Fish fillets may be substituted.

Mildred Clute,
Marquez, Tex.

STUFFED OYSTERS WITH SAUSAGE

1 pint oysters
1 pound bulk sausage
½ cup chopped fresh parsley
½ cup chopped green onion tops
½ cup chopped fresh mushrooms
4 hamburger buns, dried in oven and
    crumbled
¼ cup margarine
Juice of ½ lemon
Seasoned breadcrumbs

Drain oysters, reserving oyster liquor; chop oysters and set aside. Cook sausage slowly until browned in a greased 3-quart saucepan. Add oysters, parsley, onion, and mushrooms; reduce heat and cook 15 minutes.

Remove from heat and stir in crumbled bread, margarine, and lemon juice; mix well. Oyster liquor may be added in a small amount, if mixture is not as moist as desired. Fill about 12 oyster shells or 4 individual baking dishes; sprinkle with seasoned breadcrumbs. Place in shallow baking dish; bake at 250° for 25 to 30 minutes. Yield: 4 servings. *Dollye Leathers,*
Houma, La.

SHRIMP CREOLE

¼ cup plus 1 tablespoon shortening
¼ cup all-purpose flour
1 large onion, chopped
6 green onions, chopped
½ cup chopped green pepper
½ cup chopped celery
1 small clove garlic, minced
1 (16-ounce) can whole tomatoes
1 tablespoon Worcestershire sauce
½ teaspoon chopped fresh parsley
1 bay leaf
1 teaspoon salt
⅛ teaspoon pepper
⅛ teaspoon red pepper
3 pounds raw shrimp, peeled and deveined
Hot cooked rice

Melt shortening in a deep heavy skillet. Stir flour into shortening; cook over low heat, stirring constantly, until browned. Stir in remaining ingredients except shrimp and rice; simmer, stirring frequently, for 45 minutes. Stir in shrimp; cook 5 minutes more or until shrimp turn pink. Remove bay leaf. Serve over rice. Yield: 6 to 8 servings.   *Lori Graves,*
Murphy, N.C.

SEAFOOD CASSEROLE

¼ cup butter or margarine
⅓ cup chopped onion
¼ cup all-purpose flour
1 teaspoon salt
½ teaspoon white pepper
1 cup half-and-half
1 cup milk
2 tablespoons lemon juice
1 (6-ounce) package frozen crabmeat, thawed
    and flaked
1 cup cooked, peeled, and deveined shrimp
1 (5-ounce) can water chestnuts, drained and
    sliced
2 cups cooked rice
2 tablespoons chopped pimiento
1 cup (4 ounces) shredded Cheddar cheese,
    divided

Melt butter in a large saucepan. Sauté onion in butter until tender. Add flour, salt, and pepper; cook until bubbly. Slowly add half-and-half and milk, stirring constantly; cook until smooth and thickened. Remove from heat.

Add remaining ingredients except ½ cup cheese; stir to blend. Spoon mixture into a lightly greased 2-quart casserole; sprinkle with reserved cheese. Bake at 325° for 30 minutes. Yield: 6 to 8 servings.   *Mrs. W. K. Dunn,*
Eufaula, Ala.

TUNA CASSEROLE

3 tablespoons chopped onion
3 tablespoons chopped green pepper
1 tablespoon hot vegetable oil
1 (10¾-ounce) can tomato soup, undiluted
1 teaspoon chili powder
½ teaspoon salt
1 teaspoon Worcestershire sauce
1½ cups cooked noodles
1¼ cups (5 ounces) shredded sharp Cheddar
    cheese, divided
1 (6¾-ounce) can tuna, drained and flaked

Sauté onion and green pepper in oil in a medium saucepan. Add soup, seasonings, and Worcestershire sauce; simmer 5 minutes. Add noodles, 1 cup cheese, and tuna. Spoon into a lightly greased 1-quart casserole and bake at 350° for 30 minutes. While still hot, sprinkle with remaining cheese. Yield: 4 to 5 servings.
Jane McGuire,
Roanoke, Va.

BAKED DOVES WITH APPLE DRESSING

2 cups water
1 teaspoon salt
12 doves, cleaned
Apple Dressing

Combine water and salt in a saucepan; add doves. Cover and simmer about 15 minutes or until tender. Drain and set aside. Spoon Apple Dressing into a lightly greased oblong baking dish; arrange doves, breast side down, on top of dressing. Bake at 375° for 30 minutes or until birds are well browned. Yield: 6 servings.

APPLE DRESSING:

3 cups crumbled cornbread or breadcrumbs
2 cups peeled and chopped cooking apples
½ cup chopped celery
1 small onion, chopped
¼ cup butter or margarine, melted
½ teaspoon salt
½ teaspoon poultry seasoning
½ cup milk

Combine all ingredients in a large mixing bowl. Yield: about 5 cups.

DOVES WITH WILD RICE

10 to 12 whole dove breasts
½ teaspoon seasoned salt
½ teaspoon salt
¼ teaspoon freshly ground black pepper
1 cup water, divided
½ cup butter or margarine, melted
2 tablespoons lemon juice
1 tablespoon all-purpose flour
Cooked wild rice
Celery leaves (optional)

Wipe dove breasts with a clean, damp cloth or paper towels. Place breasts in a large iron skillet. Combine salt and pepper; sprinkle over doves.

Pour ½ cup water into the skillet; cover tightly, and steam over medium heat 20 minutes. Remove lid, and continue cooking until all water is gone.

Add butter and lemon juice to skillet. Continue cooking until breasts are brown on all sides, turning occasionally; remove breasts from skillet.

Add flour to drippings in skillet, stirring until smooth; cook over low heat until lightly browned. Add remaining ½ cup water; cook until thickened, stirring constantly. Pour gravy over breasts; serve over wild rice. Garnish with celery leaves, if desired. Yield: 4 to 6 servings.

DOVES WITH ORANGE GLAZE

12 doves, cleaned
Juice of 2 lemons (about ⅓ cup)
¾ cup Worcestershire sauce
1 teaspoon salt
Dash of pepper
6 slices bacon, halved
1 (12-ounce) can frozen orange juice concentrate, thawed and undiluted

Place doves in a large bowl. Pour lemon juice over each bird; add Worcestershire sauce, salt, and pepper. Cover tightly and marinate several hours in refrigerator, turning to marinate all sides.

Remove from marinade. Wrap each bird with bacon, securing with a toothpick. Place in a shallow roasting pan, and pour orange juice concentrate over birds. Bake at 350° for 1 hour, turning and basting birds frequently. Yield: 6 servings.

SAUCY DOVES

About 1 cup all-purpose flour
1¼ teaspoons salt
¼ teaspoon pepper
½ teaspoon poultry seasoning
12 to 15 doves, cleaned
½ cup melted butter or margarine
1 (8-ounce) can tomato sauce
1 (4-ounce) can mushroom pieces, drained
1 large onion, diced
About ⅓ cup milk

Combine flour, salt, pepper, and poultry seasoning in a bag; add doves and shake to coat birds well. Brown doves in butter in a large skillet. Add tomato sauce, mushrooms, and onion. Cover and cook over low heat until tender, about 20 minutes. Remove doves and keep warm.

Add milk to pan drippings, scraping sides and bottom of skillet. Heat, stirring constantly, to make a sauce; spoon over doves. Yield: about 6 servings.

Note: Quail may be used instead of dove.

PECAN-STUFFED WILD DUCK

4 cups soft breadcrumbs
1 cup finely chopped celery
1 cup finely chopped onion
1 cup raisins
1 cup chopped pecans
½ teaspoon salt
½ cup scalded milk
2 eggs, beaten
2 (2½-pound) wild ducks, cleaned and dressed
6 slices bacon or salt pork
1 cup catsup
¼ cup Worcestershire sauce
¼ cup steak sauce
½ cup chili sauce
Orange slices (optional)

Combine breadcrumbs, celery, onion, raisins, pecans, and salt; mix well. Add milk and eggs to dry mixture; stir well. Stuff into cavities of ducks; close with skewers. Place ducks in roaster; cover each duck with 3 strips of bacon. Roast, uncovered, at 350° for 15 to 25 minutes. Combine remaining ingredients except orange slices, mixing well. Baste ducks with sauce mixture. Bake at 350° for 20 minutes. Skim fat from sauce and serve sauce with ducks. Garnish ducks with orange slices, if desired. Yield: 4 to 6 servings.

Betty Martin,
Harrison, Ark.

SMOTHERED QUAIL

Quail
Salt and pepper
All-purpose flour
Hot vegetable oil

Pick quail clean and wash thoroughly. Salt and pepper birds inside and outside. Dredge in flour and brown on all sides in vegetable oil. Drain off excess drippings; slowly add hot water just to cover birds. Cover pan and simmer over low heat 45 to 55 minutes or until birds are tender.

VENISON, HUNTER'S STYLE

3 pounds venison
Salt and pepper
2 tablespoons butter or margarine
1 onion, chopped
1 (1-inch) cube ham, minced
1 clove garlic, minced
2 bay leaves
2 sprigs thyme, crushed
1 tablespoon all-purpose flour
2 cups warm water
4 cups consommé
½ pound fresh mushrooms, chopped
Grated rind of 1 lemon

Cut venison into pieces 2 inches square; salt and pepper generously. Heat butter in skillet and brown venison slowly. When almost brown, add onion; brown slightly. Then add ham, garlic, bay leaves, and thyme. Stir and simmer for 2 minutes. Add flour and cook a few minutes longer.

Add warm water and bring to a boil. Add consommé; reduce heat and cook slowly for 1 hour. Season again according to taste; then add mushrooms and lemon rind. Let cook 30 minutes longer. Serve on a very hot plate. Yield: 8 servings.

When Orange Baked Chicken (page 43) is complete, chicken breasts are arranged over noodles to make an attractive holiday entrée.

Overleaf: Here are two delicious vegetable salads that offer variety and color to winter menus: Confetti Potato Salad (page 59) and Broccoli and Cauliflower Salad (page 58).

Salads

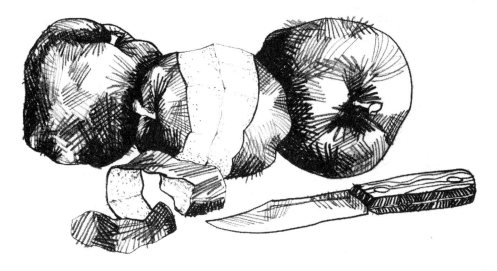

A colorful salad may be exactly what's needed to add a lift to your meals, and Southern gardens give us plenty of fresh ingredients to choose from. Yours can be as crisp as a bowl of mixed greens, as cool as a congealed aspic, or as bright as a combination of fruits.

And don't forget the menu possibilities of hearty main dish salads. Preparation is quick and easy, and these salads lend themselves well to the use of leftovers.

APPLE CIDER SALAD

1 (6-ounce) package orange-flavored gelatin
4 cups apple cider
1 cup raisins
1 cup coarsely chopped apple
1 cup chopped celery
Juice and grated rind of 1 lemon
Lettuce
1 apple, unpeeled and sliced (optional)

Dissolve gelatin in 2 cups hot apple cider; stir in raisins. Let cool.

Add remaining 2 cups cider; chill until consistency of unbeaten egg white. Stir in chopped apple, celery, lemon juice, and rind. Pour into a lightly oiled 6-cup mold. Chill until set. Unmold onto lettuce leaves and garnish with apple slices, if desired. Yield: 8 to 10 servings.   *Mrs. Charles Judy,*
Daleville, Va.

GRAPEFRUIT ASPIC

1 (3-ounce) package lemon- or lime-flavored gelatin
1 tablespoon sugar
¾ cup boiling water
1 cup unsweetened grapefruit juice
2 medium grapefruit, peeled, seeded, and sectioned
¾ cup sliced almonds
Lettuce leaves

Dissolve gelatin and sugar in boiling water; stir in grapefruit juice. Chill mixture until slightly thickened.

Chop grapefruit sections; drain. Stir grapefruit and almonds into thickened gelatin. Pour mixture into lightly oiled ⅓-cup molds. Chill until firm. Serve on lettuce leaves. Yield: 8 servings.   *Mrs. E. C. Holloway,*
Murfreesboro, Tenn.

APRICOT SALAD

2 (3-ounce) packages orange-flavored gelatin
2 cups boiling water
⅓ cup miniature marshmallows
1 (30-ounce) can apricots
1 (8¼-ounce) can crushed pineapple
2 tablespoons butter or margarine
2 tablespoons all-purpose flour
½ cup sugar
1 egg, beaten
1 cup frozen whipped topping, thawed
Chopped pecans (optional)

Dissolve gelatin in boiling water. Add marshmallows; stir until dissolved.

Drain apricots and pineapple, reserving juice. Set aside ½ cup apricot juice and ½ cup pineapple juice for topping. Combine remaining juice and add water to measure 2 cups; stir into gelatin. Chill until consistency of unbeaten egg white.

Chop apricots; fold apricots and pineapple into gelatin. Pour into a 13- x 9- x 2-inch dish. Chill until firm.

Melt butter; add flour, stirring well. Add sugar, egg, and reserved apricot and pineapple juice. Cook over medium heat until thickened. Chill. Fold in whipped topping. Spread over gelatin mixture. Sprinkle with pecans, if desired. Yield: about 15 servings.

Rachel V. Youree,
Murfreesboro, Tenn.

CRANBERRY SALAD SUPREME

1 cup chopped fresh cranberries
½ cup chopped apple
½ cup chopped nuts
⅓ cup sugar
1 (3-ounce) package orange-flavored gelatin
1¾ cups boiling water
1 envelope whipped topping mix

Combine first 4 ingredients; set aside. Dissolve gelatin in water; cool. Combine gelatin and fruit mixture; chill until slightly thickened.

Prepare topping according to package directions; fold into gelatin mixture. Pour into a 6-cup mold; chill until firm. Yield: about 10 servings.

Mrs. Russell Adams,
Rogers, Ark.

DREAMY FROZEN FRUIT SALAD

2 (1.5-ounce) envelopes whipped topping mix
2 (3-ounce) packages cream cheese, softened
¼ cup lemon juice
1 (14-ounce) can sweetened condensed milk
1 cup chopped pecans
1 (15¼-ounce) can pineapple chunks, drained
1 (21-ounce) can cherry pie filling

Prepare whipped topping mix according to package directions; set aside.

Combine cream cheese and lemon juice; beat until smooth. Stir in milk, pecans, and pineapple. Fold in whipped topping and pie filling. Spoon mixture into paper-lined muffin pans. Cover and freeze. Yield: 24 servings.

Note: Frozen salads may be removed from muffin pans and stored in plastic freezer bags.

HOLIDAY JEWEL SALAD

1 (3-ounce) package pineapple-flavored gelatin
1 cup boiling water
1 (8-ounce) can crushed pineapple
1 cup fresh cranberries, chopped
½ cup diced celery
½ cup chopped walnuts
Lettuce leaves (optional)

Dissolve gelatin in boiling water. Drain pineapple, reserving juice. Add water to juice to measure 1 cup; stir into gelatin mixture. Chill until consistency of unbeaten egg white.

Combine pineapple, cranberries, celery, and walnuts; fold into gelatin. Pour into a lightly oiled 1-quart mold; chill until firm.

Unmold on lettuce leaves, if desired. Yield: 6 to 8 servings. *Mrs. William Russell,*
Yazoo City, Miss.

LAYERED HOLIDAY SALAD

1 (3-ounce) package cherry-flavored gelatin
1½ cups boiling water
1 (3-ounce) package lemon-flavored gelatin
1½ cups boiling water
1 (3-ounce) package cream cheese, softened
1 cup whipping cream, whipped
1 (3-ounce) package lime-flavored gelatin
1 cup boiling water
1 (15¼-ounce) can crushed pineapple,
    undrained

Dissolve cherry gelatin in 1½ cups boiling water. Pour into a 12- x 7½- x 1½-inch dish. Chill until firm.

Dissolve lemon gelatin in 1½ cups boiling water. Gradually add to cream cheese, mixing until smooth. Cool. Fold in whipped cream. Pour over first layer; chill until firm.

Dissolve lime gelatin in 1 cup boiling water. Chill until consistency of unbeaten egg white. Stir pineapple into gelatin; pour over cream cheese layer. Chill until firm. Cut into squares to serve. Yield: 12 servings.

Marmell O'Brien,
Clay, W. Va.

HEAVENLY SALAD

1 egg, beaten
1 tablespoon sugar
1 tablespoon orange juice
1 tablespoon vinegar
1½ teaspoons butter or margarine
Dash of salt
1 cup commercial sour cream
1 cup seedless green grapes
1 cup sliced banana
1 cup diced pineapple
1 (16-ounce) can pitted bing cherries, drained
1 cup maraschino cherries, drained
1 cup diced orange
1 (10-ounce) package frozen mixed fruit,
    thawed and drained
2 cups miniature marshmallows
Flaked coconut

Combine first 4 ingredients in a saucepan; mix well. Cook over medium heat until thickened, stirring constantly. Remove from heat. Add butter and salt; stir until butter melts. Chill. Fold in sour cream.

Combine remaining ingredients except coconut. Fold in dressing. Sprinkle coconut over top. Chill. Yield: 10 to 12 servings.

Janice Finn,
Greensburg, Ky.

FROSTED STRAWBERRY SALAD

1 (6-ounce) package strawberry gelatin
2 cups boiling water
1 cup cold water
1 (20-ounce) can crushed pineapple
1 (10-ounce) package frozen strawberries,
    thawed
2 bananas, peeled and sliced
1 cup miniature marshmallows
2 tablespoons all-purpose flour
½ cup sugar
⅛ teaspoon salt
2 teaspoons butter or margarine
1 (1½-ounce) package whipped topping mix
½ cup chopped pecans
½ cup plus 1 tablespoon shredded coconut,
    divided

Dissolve gelatin in boiling water, and stir in cold water. Drain pineapple, reserving 1 cup juice. Stir in pineapple, strawberries, bananas, and marshmallows. Pour mixture into a 9-inch square pan; chill until firm.

Combine flour, sugar, and salt in a small saucepan; add reserved pineapple juice and butter. Cook over medium heat until mixture reaches a boil and thickens. Remove from heat; let cool completely.

Prepare whipped topping mix according to package directions. Fold in cooled juice mixture, pecans, and ½ cup coconut. Spread mixture over chilled gelatin; top with remaining coconut. Chill. Yield: 9 servings.

Mrs. Lyman Clayborn,
Kinston, N.C.

Fruit Salads 55

MEXICAN CHEF SALAD

1 pound lean ground beef
1 (15-ounce) can kidney beans, drained
1 teaspoon salt
1 head lettuce, chopped
1 medium onion, chopped
4 medium tomatoes, chopped
1 cup (4 ounces) shredded Cheddar cheese
1 (8-ounce) package tortilla chips, crushed
1 large avocado, peeled, seeded, and sliced
Commercial salad dressing (optional)

Cook ground beef until brown, stirring to crumble. Drain excess fat from skillet. Add beans and salt, stirring well; simmer 10 minutes.

Combine lettuce, onion, tomatoes, cheese, and tortilla chips. Add beef mixture; toss lightly. Garnish with avocado. Serve with salad dressing, if desired. Yield: 8 to 10 servings.

Sylvia Stephens,
New Hill, N.C.

CONFETTI MACARONI SALAD

1 (8-ounce) package or 2 cups elbow
    macaroni
1 (12-ounce) can luncheon meat, diced
1½ cups diced Cheddar cheese
½ cup chopped green pepper
⅓ cup chopped onion
½ cup mayonnaise
2 tablespoons milk
2 tablespoons vinegar
½ teaspoon salt
Lettuce

Cook macaroni according to the package directions; drain well. Combine macaroni, luncheon meat, cheese, green pepper, and onion; stir well and chill.

Combine mayonnaise, milk, vinegar, and salt; pour over macaroni salad, and toss well. Serve in lettuce-lined bowl. Yield: 10 to 12 servings.

Pauline Lester,
Saluda, S.C.

HOT CHICKEN OR TURKEY SALAD

4 cups diced cooked chicken or turkey
1 teaspoon salt
1 cup diced celery
¾ cup chopped almonds
¾ cup chopped green pepper
1 cup mayonnaise
1 (10¾-ounce) can cream of chicken soup,
    undiluted
4 hard-cooked eggs, chopped
¾ cup crushed potato chips

Combine all ingredients except potato chips; place in a greased 2½-quart casserole. Top with potato chips. Bake at 350° for 25 minutes. Yield: 8 servings.

Mary Conger,
Fayetteville, Tenn.

RICE AND SHRIMP SALAD

3 cups unsalted cooked rice, cooled
½ cup finely chopped onion
½ cup finely chopped sweet pickle
¼ cup diced pimiento
½ pound shrimp, cooked, peeled, and
    deveined
4 hard-cooked eggs, chopped
¾ to 1 cup mayonnaise
1 teaspoon salt
¼ teaspoon pepper
1 teaspoon prepared mustard
Lettuce
Tomato wedges (optional)
Ripe olives (optional)

Combine first 10 ingredients and toss lightly; chill thoroughly. Serve on lettuce leaves; garnish with tomato wedges and olives, if desired. Yield: 6 to 8 servings.

Note: 1 (7-ounce) can tuna, drained and flaked, or 1½ cups finely chopped cooked chicken, beef, or pork may be substituted for shrimp.

Laura King,
Lancaster, Tex.

VEGETABLE-SHRIMP SALAD

1 (10-ounce) package frozen cauliflower
1 (10-ounce) package frozen brussels sprouts
1 (10-ounce) package frozen broccoli spears
1 (10-ounce) package frozen lima beans
1 pound cooked, peeled, and deveined shrimp
1 cup whole pitted ripe olives
¼ cup chopped pimiento
1 cup lemon juice
½ cup vegetable oil
2 tablespoons chopped parsley
2 teaspoons salt
1 teaspoon monosodium glutamate
1 teaspoon whole basil
Lettuce leaves (optional)

Cook each vegetable separately; follow package directions, but cook 3 minutes or until vegetables are crisp-tender. Drain and cool.

Cut cauliflower into small flowerets. Cut brussels sprouts in half lengthwise; cut broccoli in half crosswise.

Combine vegetables, shrimp, olives, and pimiento in a large bowl; toss lightly, and set aside.

Combine next 6 ingredients, mixing well. Pour dressing over vegetables; toss lightly to coat. Cover and chill thoroughly. Toss again before serving. Serve on lettuce leaves, if desired. Yield: 6 to 8 servings.

CRAB AND WILD RICE SALAD

½ (4-ounce) package wild rice
2 (6-ounce) packages frozen crabmeat, thawed, drained, and flaked
1 (6-ounce) package frozen, cooked shrimp, thawed
½ cup cooked English peas, drained
½ cup chopped onion
2 tablespoons chopped pimiento
½ cup mayonnaise
1 tablespoon lemon juice
1 teaspoon curry powder
Lettuce
Cherry tomatoes or tomato wedges

Cook rice according to package directions. Combine rice, crabmeat, shrimp, peas, onion, and pimiento; stir lightly.

Combine mayonnaise, lemon juice, and curry powder; stir into crab mixture. Cover and chill. Serve on lettuce leaves; garnish with tomatoes. Yield: 5 servings.

TUNA-RICE SALAD

1 (6-ounce) package chicken-flavored vermicelli-rice mix
1 (7-ounce) can tuna, drained and flaked
½ cup sliced green onion
½ cup chopped celery
1 cup chopped tomato
2 tablespoons wine vinegar
2 tablespoons lemon juice
1 tablespoon sugar
⅛ teaspoon garlic powder
Green pepper rings (optional)
Parsley sprigs (optional)

Prepare rice mix according to package directions. Cool. Add tuna, onion, celery, and tomato, tossing lightly.

Combine vinegar, lemon juice, sugar, and garlic powder, stirring well; pour over rice mixture. Toss mixture well, and garnish with green pepper rings and parsley, if desired. Chill before serving. Yield: 6 servings.

Mary Ann Banks,
Decatur, Ga.

Tip: To keep such foods as pork chops, strawberries, or diced green pepper from sticking together while freezing, place in a single layer on a cookie sheet and freeze until solid. Then remove from cookie sheet, and store in freezer bags or containers.

BROCCOLI AND CAULIFLOWER SALAD

1 pound fresh cauliflower, chopped
1 pound fresh broccoli, chopped
1 small onion, chopped
⅓ cup vinegar
⅓ cup sugar
⅔ cup mayonnaise
1 teaspoon salt

Combine cauliflower, broccoli, and onion; toss well. Combine remaining ingredients, mixing well; pour over vegetables. Let stand in refrigerator overnight. Yield: 6 to 8 servings.
Mrs. Forest Lundy,
Choctaw, Okla.

OLD-FASHIONED CABBAGE SALAD

4 cups finely shredded cabbage
¼ cup chopped green pepper
1 tablespoon chopped pimiento
1 teaspoon instant minced onion
⅓ cup vinegar
3 tablespoons vegetable oil
2 tablespoons sugar
1 teaspoon salt
½ teaspoon dry mustard
½ teaspoon celery seeds
¼ teaspoon pepper
Watercress (optional)
Sliced pimiento-stuffed olives (optional)

Combine all ingredients except watercress and olives in a large bowl; mix well.
Cover and refrigerate at least 3 hours. Drain before serving. Garnish with watercress and sliced olives, if desired. Yield: 6 servings.
Mrs. Gary Ferguson,
Dallas, Tex.

Tip: Freshen wilted vegetables by letting them stand about 10 minutes in cold water to which a few drops of lemon juice have been added; drain well, and store in a plastic bag in the refrigerator.

GARDEN GLORY COLESLAW

3 cups shredded green cabbage
2 cups shredded red cabbage
1 cup shredded carrot
⅓ cup finely chopped green pepper
2 green onions, thinly sliced
2 tablespoons tarragon vinegar
1 tablespoon sugar
1 teaspoon salt
½ cup mayonnaise
Tomato wedges

Combine cabbage, carrot, green pepper, and onion in a medium bowl; toss well.
Combine vinegar, sugar, and salt in a small mixing bowl; gradually stir vinegar mixture into mayonnaise, mixing well. Stir mayonnaise mixture into vegetable mixture, mixing well. Cover and chill at least 1 hour. Garnish with tomato wedges before serving. Yield: 6 servings.
Mrs. Eva G. Key,
Isle of Palms, S.C.

ENGLISH PEA GARDEN SALAD

1 medium cucumber, chopped
1 stalk celery, chopped
1 large carrot, chopped
1 green pepper, chopped
2 medium tomatoes, chopped
2 to 3 green onions, chopped, or 1 medium onion, chopped
2 hard-cooked eggs, chopped
Salt and pepper to taste
1 (17-ounce) can English peas, drained
¾ to 1 cup mayonnaise or salad dressing
Lettuce (optional)

Combine first 7 ingredients in a large bowl; add salt and pepper, stirring gently. Add peas and mayonnaise, stirring gently. Refrigerate until thoroughly chilled. Serve on lettuce leaves, if desired. Yield: 8 to 10 servings.
Mary R. Logan,
Kingsport, Tenn.

OVERNIGHT BLACK-EYED PEA SALAD

2 (15-ounce) cans black-eyed peas with snaps, drained
½ cup thinly sliced red onion, separated into rings
½ cup chopped green pepper
½ clove garlic
¼ cup sugar
¼ cup vinegar
¼ cup vegetable oil
½ teaspoon salt
Dash of pepper
Dash of hot sauce

Combine peas, onion, and green pepper in a medium bowl. Stick a toothpick through the garlic; add to vegetables.

Combine remaining ingredients, stirring well. Add to vegetable mixture, tossing lightly to coat. Cover; refrigerate for at least 12 hours. Remove toothpick with garlic before serving. Yield: 6 to 8 servings.   *Mrs. J. W. Hopkins,*
Abilene, Tex.

THREE BEAN SALAD

1 (15½-ounce) can cut green beans, drained
1 (15½-ounce) can cut wax beans, drained
1 (15-ounce) can red kidney beans, drained
1 green pepper, chopped
1 onion, chopped
⅔ cup vinegar
¾ cup sugar
⅓ cup vegetable oil
1 teaspoon salt
½ teaspoon pepper
Onion slices

Combine beans, green pepper, and onion in a large bowl and toss lightly. Combine remaining ingredients except onion slices and pour over tossed vegetables. Cover and refrigerate overnight. Garnish with onion slices. Yield: 10 servings.   *Chelsa Dickerson,*
Hoboken, Ga.

CONFETTI POTATO SALAD

10 medium potatoes, peeled and cubed
1 to 1½ cups mayonnaise or salad dressing
2 tablespoons vinegar
1½ teaspoons salt
¼ teaspoon pepper
6 hard-cooked eggs, chopped
3 medium tomatoes, chopped
1 cup celery, chopped
¾ cup green pepper, chopped
¼ cup onion, chopped

Cook potatoes in a small amount of boiling, salted water until tender. Drain well and mash until smooth. Add mayonnaise, vinegar, salt, and pepper; mix well. Add remaining ingredients; stir gently to mix well. Serve warm or cold. Yield: 12 servings.   *June Bostick,*
Fruitland, Md.

RASPBERRY-TOMATO MOLD

2 (3-ounce) packages raspberry-flavored gelatin
2 cups boiling water
¼ teaspoon lemon juice
1 tablespoon Worcestershire sauce
1 tablespoon plus 1½ teaspoons prepared horseradish
2 cups stewed tomatoes, chopped
Lettuce
Mayonnaise (optional)

Combine gelatin and water; stir until gelatin dissolves. Add lemon juice, Worcestershire sauce, horseradish, and tomatoes; mix well. Pour into a lightly oiled 1-quart mold; chill until firm. Unmold on lettuce and top with mayonnaise, if desired. Yield: 6 servings.

Margaret Corn,
Lonoke, Ark.

PIQUANT VEGETABLE SALAD

1 (10-ounce) package frozen succotash, cooked and drained
1 (15½-ounce) can kidney beans, rinsed and drained
2 cups thinly sliced celery
2 cups thinly sliced fresh mushrooms
2 green onions, chopped
½ cup ripe olives, sliced
½ cup commercial Italian salad dressing
1 (9-ounce) package hot pepper process cheese, diced (about 2 cups)
Parsley sprigs (optional)

Combine vegetables, olives, and Italian salad dressing in a large bowl; toss lightly. Refrigerate 1½ to 2 hours. Add cheese; toss lightly. Garnish with parsley, if desired; serve at once. Yield: 10 to 12 servings. *Johnetta Hall, Currie, N.C.*

VEGETABLE CONGEALED SALAD

1½ tablespoons unflavored gelatin
½ cup cold water
1 (10¾-ounce) can tomato soup, undiluted
2 (3-ounce) packages cream cheese, softened
1 cup mayonnaise
1 green pepper, finely chopped
1 medium onion, finely chopped
⅔ cup finely chopped celery
⅔ cup sliced pimiento-stuffed olives

Dissolve gelatin in cold water. Heat soup, stirring until smooth. Stir in gelatin. Beat cream cheese, and add 2 to 3 tablespoons tomato soup mixture, beating until smooth; blend into soup mixture. Cool. Stir in remaining ingredients. Pour into a 9-inch square pan. Refrigerate until firm. Yield: about 9 servings.

Mrs. Artie B. Lowe, Milledgeville, Ga.

MARINATED VEGETABLE SALAD

1 (17-ounce) can small English peas, drained
1 (17-ounce) can white shoe peg corn, drained
1 (15½-ounce) can French-style green beans, drained
1 (2-ounce) jar diced pimiento, drained
½ cup diced celery
½ to 1 cup chopped onion
½ cup chopped green pepper
1 cup sugar
½ teaspoon pepper
1 teaspoon salt
½ cup vegetable oil
¾ cup vinegar

Combine vegetables, tossing lightly. Combine remaining ingredients in a medium saucepan; bring to a boil over low heat, stirring occasionally. Pour over vegetables, stirring gently to blend well. Cover and chill 24 hours. Yield: 6 to 8 servings. *Mrs. Roger L. Grace, White Plains, Ky.*

SPINACH AND EGG SALAD

4 cups torn fresh spinach
4 hard-cooked eggs, quartered
4 bacon slices, cooked and crumbled
½ cup mayonnaise
¼ cup chili sauce
1 tablespoon grated onion

Combine spinach, eggs, and bacon in a large bowl.
Combine mayonnaise, chili sauce, and onion; mix well. Serve over spinach. Yield: 4 servings. *Florence L. Costello, Chattanooga, Tenn.*

This delicious Raspberry Tomato Mold (page 59) will be a colorful addition to your dinner table.

Overleaf: *Long, slow cooking in the oven gives Savory Beef Stew (page 66) a rich, hearty flavor the family will enjoy.*

Soups and Stews

Savory, mouth-watering soups and stews are favorites throughout the South. Each has its own special combination of meats, seafood, vegetables, and seasonings, and many of them need not simmer for hours to be good.

Soups range from cool appetizers to filling main dish selections. Stews are hot and hearty and have a way of warming you up when it's cold outside. Many can be made the day before serving and may have an even better flavor after standing.

CHICKEN SOUP

1 (2½- to 3-pound) broiler-fryer, cut up
1 tablespoon salt
½ cup butter or margarine
About 1 quart boiling water
1 large potato, peeled and cubed
1 medium onion, coarsely chopped
2 (17-ounce) cans cream-style corn
1 (28-ounce) can tomatoes, undrained
½ teaspoon pepper

Combine chicken, salt, butter, and boiling water in a Dutch oven. Bring to a boil; reduce heat and simmer until chicken is tender.

Remove chicken from broth. Cool and remove meat from bones; set aside. Add potato and onion to broth. Bring to a boil; reduce heat and cook until vegetables are tender. Add chicken and remaining ingredients to broth. Simmer 30 to 45 minutes, stirring occasionally. Yield: about 8 servings.   *Pauline Horn,*
Carthage, Miss.

GAZPACHO

2 cups finely chopped tomato
1 cup finely chopped celery
1 cup finely chopped green pepper
1 cup finely chopped cucumber
1 cup sliced green onion
1 (4-ounce) can chopped green chiles, rinsed
    and drained
2 (8-ounce) cans tomato sauce
½ to 1 cup water
¼ cup vinegar
¼ cup vegetable oil
3 to 4 teaspoons salt
2 teaspoons Worcestershire sauce

Combine vegetables and chiles in a large bowl. Combine remaining ingredients; beat until blended well. Pour over vegetables and toss lightly. Cover and chill 6 to 8 hours. Stir gently before serving. Yield: 6 to 8 servings.
Mrs. John Mosley,
Franklin, Ariz.

CREAM OF CUCUMBER SOUP

2 cups peeled and sliced cucumber
¼ cup chopped celery
1 cup chicken broth or chicken bouillon
1 cup milk or half-and-half
3 tablespoons butter or margarine, melted
2 tablespoons all-purpose flour

Combine all ingredients in container of electric blender; blend until smooth. Chill 3 to 4 hours. Yield: 4 to 6 servings.

Note: Soup may be served hot; sprinkle with dillweed, if desired.   *Nell Little,*
Jonesboro, Tenn.

LENTIL-VEGETABLE SOUP

1 cup dried lentils
4 cups water
½ cup chopped onion
½ cup thinly sliced celery
½ cup diced carrots
1 bay leaf
1 clove garlic, minced
1 teaspoon salt
⅛ teaspoon pepper
2 frankfurters, thinly sliced
Lemon slices, quartered

Rinse lentils; drain and place in Dutch oven. Add water, onion, celery, carrots, bay leaf, garlic, salt, and pepper. Cover and simmer for 2 hours. Remove bay leaf. Add frankfurters; heat for 5 minutes. Garnish each serving with lemon. Yield: 4 servings.   *C. Jobe,*
Tahlequah, Okla.

VEGETABLE-HAM SOUP

1½ cups dried navy or baby lima beans
1 (3-pound) meaty ham bone
3 quarts water
1½ cups coarsely chopped carrots
1½ cups coarsely chopped potatoes
1 large onion, chopped
½ teaspoon salt
¼ teaspoon pepper

Rinse and soak beans; combine beans, ham bone, and water in a large Dutch oven. Bring to a boil; reduce heat, cover, and simmer for 3 to 3¼ hours or until beans are tender. Remove ham bone and chop meat coarsely; discard bone. Add ham and remaining ingredients to beans; simmer 30 minutes or until vegetables are tender, stirring occasionally. Yield: 8 to 10 servings.   *Mrs. K. M. Roach,*
Jacksonville Beach, Fla.

OLD-FASHIONED SPLIT PEA SOUP

1½ cups dried split peas
1 ham bone, turkey carcass, or 2-inch cube salt pork
1 medium onion, sliced
11 slices lemon
½ cup chopped carrots
1 cup chopped celery and leaves
6 cups cold water
Salt
Pepper
Paprika

Wash peas and put in a Dutch oven; add ham bone, onion, 3 lemon slices, carrots, celery, and water. Simmer over low heat for 6 hours. Discard ham bone and lemon slices.

Skim off surface fat and put soup through a coarse strainer. Return soup to Dutch oven and season with salt and pepper. Heat thoroughly. Garnish each serving with a lemon slice and a dash of paprika. Yield: 8 servings.

POTATO SOUP

4 medium potatoes, peeled and finely chopped
2 tablespoons chopped onion
2 tablespoons chopped celery
4 cups milk
¼ cup butter or margarine, softened
Salt and pepper to taste
Chopped parsley

Barely cover potatoes, onion, and celery with water; cook until tender. Mash with potato masher. Add milk, butter, salt, and pepper. Cook until thoroughly heated. Serve topped with parsley. Yield: 4 servings.

PORTUGUESE SOUP

1½ pounds Portuguese or Polish sausage, sliced
5 cups water, divided
2 (15-ounce) cans kidney beans, drained
2 carrots, diced
½ head cabbage, coarsely chopped
1 medium onion, chopped
2 medium potatoes, diced
½ green pepper, chopped
1 clove garlic, finely chopped
1 (8-ounce) can tomato sauce

Simmer sausage in 2 cups water for 30 to 45 minutes in a Dutch oven. Add remaining ingredients and simmer 1 to 1½ hours. Yield: 10 servings.

SAUSAGE AND BEAN SOUP

1 pound Great Northern beans
1 large onion, chopped
1 teaspoon garlic salt
3 pounds smoked sausage, cut into ¼-inch slices
1 pound carrots, peeled and shredded
1 (5-ounce) can pimientos, drained and mashed
2 large potatoes, peeled and diced
1 (8-ounce) can tomato sauce
2 cups water

Sort beans and wash thoroughly; cover with water and soak overnight. Drain beans and place in a large, heavy Dutch oven; add onion and garlic salt. Cover with water and bring to a boil. Reduce heat; cover and simmer 1 hour.

Stir in remaining ingredients; cover and simmer 1 hour, stirring occasionally. Yield: 14 to 16 servings. *Mrs. Don Everett, Marshall, Tex.*

OLD-FASHIONED SUPPER SOUP

½ cup chopped onion
1 clove garlic, minced
1 teaspoon dried basil leaves
2 tablespoons margarine, melted
2 (10¾-ounce) cans golden mushroom soup, undiluted
2⅔ cups water
1 (16-ounce) can stewed tomatoes, chopped
2 cups diced cooked chicken or turkey
1½ cups medium egg noodles, uncooked

Sauté onion, garlic, and basil in margarine in a large, heavy saucepan. Cook until tender. Stir in soup and water; add remaining ingredients. Bring to a boil; reduce heat. Cook 10 minutes or until noodles are done; stir occasionally. Yield: 6 to 8 servings.

TURKEY-CORN CHOWDER

1 medium onion, chopped
¼ cup butter or margarine, melted
2 cups water
2 chicken bouillon cubes
3 cups diced cooked turkey or chicken
1 cup sliced celery
5 medium potatoes, peeled and cubed
1 (17-ounce) can golden whole kernel corn, drained
1 (17-ounce) can golden cream-style corn
1 quart milk
Salt and pepper to taste
Chopped fresh parsley (optional)
Paprika (optional)

Sauté onion in butter in a Dutch oven until tender. Add water, bouillon cubes, turkey, celery, and potatoes; cook 20 to 30 minutes or until potatoes are tender. Add corn, milk, and salt and pepper to taste; simmer until hot. Sprinkle with parsley and paprika, if desired. Yield: 8 to 10 servings. *Thelma Olson, Lexington, Okla.*

CHUNKY CORN AND HAM CHOWDER

3 tablespoons margarine
1 cup diced celery
¾ cup chopped onion
2 tablespoons all-purpose flour
2 cups milk
1 cup water
1 pound cooked ham, cut into ½-inch cubes
⅛ teaspoon pepper
⅛ teaspoon ground nutmeg
1 (17-ounce) can whole kernel corn, drained
¼ cup chopped parsley

Melt margarine in a large saucepan; sauté celery and onion for 2 minutes. Add flour; cook, stirring constantly, for 2 minutes. Gradually add milk and water, stirring until smooth and thickened. Add ham, pepper, nutmeg, and corn. Bring to a boil; reduce heat, cover, and simmer 10 minutes. Garnish with parsley before serving. Yield: 6 to 8 servings.

Marlene Miller,
Trenton, Fla.

BAKED STEW

2½ pounds lean beef for stewing
4 large potatoes, cut into 1-inch pieces
6 carrots, cut into ½-inch pieces
1 onion, diced
1 cup sliced celery
3 tablespoons quick-cooking tapioca
2 cups canned tomatoes or tomato juice
1 cup water
1 teaspoon sugar
2 teaspoons salt
Pepper to taste

Combine all ingredients in a heavy Dutch oven. Cover and bake at 300° for 3 to 3½ hours or until done. Yield: 8 servings.

Note: Stew may be baked at 250° for 3½ to 5 hours, if desired. *Nina Ward,*
Caldwell, Kans.

SAVORY BEEF STEW

2 pounds lean beef for stewing, cut into 1-inch cubes
¼ cup vegetable oil
1½ cups chopped onion
1 (16-ounce) can tomatoes, undrained and chopped
3 tablespoons quick-cooking tapioca
3 beef bouillon cubes
1 cup water
1 clove garlic, minced
1 tablespoon dried parsley flakes
2½ teaspoons salt
½ teaspoon pepper
1 bay leaf
6 medium carrots, cut into 2-inch strips
3 medium potatoes, cut into quarters
½ cup sliced celery

Slowly brown meat in oil in a large skillet. Add onion, tomatoes, tapioca, bouillon cubes, water, garlic, parsley, salt, pepper, and bay leaf; bring to a boil. Remove from skillet and place in a 3-quart casserole. Cover and bake at 350° for 1½ hours.

Add remaining ingredients and continue to bake for 30 to 45 minutes or until vegetables are tender. Yield: 5 to 6 servings.

Mrs. Robert W. McNeil,
Ronceverte, W. Va.

BEEFY VEGETABLE STEW

1 pound boneless beef brisket
2 pounds lean boneless beef
1 (10-ounce) package frozen whole kernel corn
1 (10-ounce) package frozen small butter beans
4 medium potatoes, peeled and cut into 1-inch cubes
2 medium onions, quartered
5 medium carrots, peeled and cut into 1-inch slices
2 (28-ounce) cans whole tomatoes, undrained
1 teaspoon salt
¼ teaspoon pepper

Cut meat into bite-size pieces; place in an 8-quart Dutch oven and cover with water. Bring to a boil; cover, reduce heat, and simmer about 1 hour.

Add remaining ingredients and simmer about 1½ hours. Yield: 12 servings.

Sara A. McCullough,
Louisville, Miss.

SPICY BEEF STEW

1¼ pounds boneless round steak, cut into bite-size pieces
1 quart canned tomatoes, undrained
1 cup peeled and sliced carrots
½ cup frozen lima beans
2 large onions, quartered
1 cup fresh cut green beans
½ cup canned English peas
½ cup cut corn
½ cup diced celery
½ cup sliced okra
1 quart tomato juice
4 cups diced potatoes
2 to 4 teaspoons hot sauce
1 teaspoon salt
¼ teaspoon pepper

Combine steak and tomatoes in a large Dutch oven; bring to a boil. Cover; reduce heat and simmer for 1 hour.

Add remaining ingredients; bring to a boil. Reduce heat and simmer, uncovered, for 1 hour, stirring occasionally. Yield: 12 servings.

Dora Smith,
Mulberry, Ark.

BRUNSWICK STEW

1 (4- to 5-pound) hen
8 cups water
3 pounds beef stew meat, cut in 1-inch cubes
1 (8-ounce) can tomato sauce
4 cups cooked tomatoes or 2 (16-ounce) cans whole tomatoes, quartered
3 medium onions, thinly sliced
3 cups diced potatoes
3 cups fresh corn or 2 (10-ounce) packages frozen whole kernel corn, thawed
2 cups fresh lima beans or 2 (10-ounce) packages frozen lima beans, thawed
½ cup butter or margarine
2 tablespoons sugar
1 tablespoon Worcestershire sauce
2 pods red pepper or dash of red pepper
1½ tablespoons salt
½ teaspoon pepper
¼ cup all-purpose flour
½ cup water

Place chicken and 8 cups water in a large Dutch oven; bring to a boil. Lower heat; cover and simmer until tender. Cool; remove meat from bones and cut into 1-inch cubes. Return to chicken broth.

Cover beef with water in a large saucepan; cook until tender. Add beef and beef broth to chicken mixture. Add tomato sauce, vegetables, butter, sugar, Worcestershire sauce, red pepper, salt, and pepper. Cover and simmer until vegetables are tender.

Combine flour and ½ cup water; mix thoroughly. Stir flour mixture into stew; cook until thickened. Yield: 16 to 20 servings.

Charlene Oden,
Haleyville, Ala.

Tip: When adding vegetables to homemade soup, remember that all vegetables should not be added at the same time. Vegetables that take the longest cooking time should be added first. These include green beans, potatoes (unless diced very thin), and corn. Canned vegetables need only to be heated, so add them last.

IRISH STEW

½ cup all-purpose flour
2 teaspoons salt
½ teaspoon paprika
1½ pounds boneless lamb, cut into 1-inch cubes
2 tablespoons butter or margarine, melted
1 cup diced onion
4 medium potatoes, peeled and thinly sliced
4 medium carrots, cut into 1-inch slices
1 tablespoon chopped parsley
1½ cups beef bouillon

Combine flour, salt, and paprika; dredge lamb in flour mixture, reserving 1 tablespoon of excess mixture. Brown lamb in butter in a large Dutch oven; remove lamb. Sauté onion in meat drippings until tender. Add lamb, potatoes, carrots, and parsley. Stir in reserved flour mixture and beef bouillon. Cover and bake at 350° for 1 hour; remove cover and bake 15 minutes longer or until the lamb is tender. Yield: 4 to 6 servings.
Helen B. Williams,
Abilene, Tex.

VEGETABLE-HAMBURGER STEW

1 pound ground beef
1 quart canned tomatoes, undrained
1 cup cut corn
1 cup sliced okra
1 (10-ounce) package frozen butter beans
4 medium potatoes, peeled and quartered
1 medium onion, quartered
¼ cup sugar
½ cup butter or margarine
1 teaspoon salt
¼ teaspoon pepper

Cook ground beef until browned in a large Dutch oven; drain off excess drippings. Stir in remaining ingredients; bring to a boil. Reduce heat and simmer about 1 hour and 15 minutes. Yield: 8 servings.
Mrs. Earl Jackson,
Preston, Miss.

MEATBALL STEW

1½ pounds ground beef
1 cup soft breadcrumbs
¼ cup chopped onion
1 egg, beaten
1 teaspoon salt
½ teaspoon dried marjoram leaves or oregano leaves
¼ teaspoon ground thyme
2 tablespoons vegetable oil
1 (10¾-ounce) can tomato soup, undiluted
1 (10½-ounce) can beef broth
1 (16-ounce) can tomatoes (optional)
8 small potatoes, cooked and drained
4 carrots, quartered
8 small onions
Chopped parsley

Combine meat, breadcrumbs, onion, egg, salt, marjoram, and thyme; shape into meatballs. Heat oil in a large skillet and brown meatballs; drain and remove from skillet. Combine soup in skillet; add meatballs and vegetables. Bring to a boil. Reduce heat; cover and simmer 30 minutes or until done. Sprinkle with parsley. Yield: 6 to 8 servings.
DaNelle Garrison,
Selma, Ala.

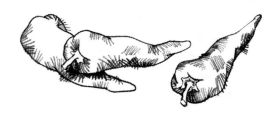

HOT CHILI

4 pounds ground beef
1 large onion, chopped
2 cloves garlic, minced
1 teaspoon dried oregano leaves
1 teaspoon ground cumin
6 tablespoons chili powder
1 tablespoon salt
2 (10-ounce) cans tomatoes and green chiles
2 cups hot water

Combine beef, onion, and garlic in a large skillet. Cook until meat is lightly browned. Drain any excess drippings. Add remaining ingredients and bring to a boil. Reduce heat and simmer 1 hour. Yield: 8 to 10 servings.

Pat Jones,
Calhoun, Ga.

EASY CHILI

1 pound ground beef
2 medium onions, chopped
1 (10-ounce) can tomatoes with green chiles
1 (8-ounce) can tomato sauce
2 teaspoons chili powder
1 teaspoon salt
⅛ teaspoon paprika
⅛ teaspoon cayenne pepper
1 (15-ounce) can red beans, drained

Cook beef and onion in large skillet until beef is browned; drain. Add tomatoes, tomato sauce, and seasonings; bring to a boil. Cover and reduce heat; simmer 1½ hours, stirring occasionally. Add beans and simmer an additional 10 minutes. Yield: 4 servings.

Mrs. A. Z. Gaines,
Stockton, Mo.

CHICKEN AND MACARONI STEW

¼ cup all-purpose flour
2 teaspoons paprika
1 teaspoon salt
½ teaspoon pepper
3 pounds chicken pieces
¼ cup vegetable oil
2 teaspoons poultry seasoning
2 cloves garlic
¼ teaspoon red pepper sauce
1 cup water
1 (28-ounce) can tomatoes, undrained
1 (10-ounce) package frozen English peas
2 medium onions, sliced
1 cup uncooked macaroni
1 teaspoon salt

Combine flour, paprika, 1 teaspoon salt, and pepper; dredge chicken with mixture. Heat oil in a large skillet and brown chicken. Add remaining ingredients; simmer about 45 minutes or until macaroni is tender. Yield: 6 to 8 servings.

Bessie Webb,
Allisonia, Va.

VEGETABLE STEW

6 slices bacon
4 medium-size green peppers, cut into strips
1 large onion, coarsely chopped
1 small clove garlic, minced
¼ pound pepperoni, cut into small pieces
2 (8-ounce) cans tomato sauce
2 cups hot water
3 large new potatoes, cut into eighths
2 yellow squash, cut into ½-inch slices
1 small (about ½-pound) eggplant, quartered lengthwise and cut into ¼-inch slices
1 teaspoon salt
¼ teaspoon pepper
Grated Parmesan cheese

Cook bacon, reserving drippings; crumble and set aside. Cook green pepper in 1 tablespoon bacon drippings about 5 minutes in a Dutch oven, stirring occasionally. Remove and set aside.

Sauté onion, garlic, and pepperoni in 1 tablespoon bacon drippings about 5 minutes, stirring occasionally. Add tomato sauce and water; simmer about 20 minutes, stirring occasionally. Add potatoes; cover and simmer about 15 minutes or until almost tender. Add squash and eggplant; simmer 10 minutes. Add green pepper and simmer 5 minutes. Season with salt and pepper. To serve, sprinkle with bacon and cheese. Yield: 6 servings.

Mrs. Kenneth B. Waldron,
Mountain Rest, S.C.

Tip: Wash most vegetables; trim any wilted parts or excess leaves before storing in crisper compartment of refrigerator. Keep potatoes and onions in a cool, dark place with plenty of air circulation to prevent sprouting.

CATFISH STEW

½ cup chopped bacon
1 cup chopped onion
1 (28-ounce) can tomatoes, undrained
2 cups diced potatoes
1 cup water
¼ cup catsup
2 tablespoons Worcestershire sauce
1 teaspoon salt
¼ teaspoon pepper
¼ teaspoon dried thyme leaves
1 pound catfish fillets, skinned and cut into
   1-inch pieces

Fry bacon until transparent; add onion and sauté until bacon is brown and onion is tender. Add remaining ingredients except fish. Reduce heat; cover and simmer 30 minutes. Add fish; cover and simmer 15 minutes or until potatoes are tender. Yield: 6 servings. *Marlene Miller, Trenton, Fla.*

FISHERMAN'S STEW

1 cup small white potatoes, diced
1 cup thinly sliced celery
2 tablespoons butter or margarine, melted
2 (10½-ounce) cans oyster stew, undiluted
2 (7-ounce) cans tuna, drained and flaked
1 (17-ounce) can English peas, drained
3 cups milk
2 tablespoons diced onion
1 teaspoon salt
2 tablespoons chopped fresh parsley
Pinch of red pepper
Additional chopped fresh parsley (optional)

Sauté potatoes and celery in butter in a large Dutch oven until potatoes are lightly browned and celery is tender. Stir in remaining ingredients except additional parsley. Heat thoroughly over medium-low heat, stirring occasionally. Garnish each serving with chopped fresh parsley, if desired. Yield: 8 to 10 servings.
Nancy Monroe,
Elizabethtown, N.C.

SHRIMP STEW

3 cups water
1 pound fresh shrimp
½ teaspoon seafood seasoning
4 slices bacon, diced
1 large onion, chopped
1 green pepper, chopped
1 stalk celery, chopped
2 tablespoons all-purpose flour
¼ cup cold water
¾ cup hot water

Bring 3 cups water to a boil; add shrimp and seafood seasoning. Return to a boil. Lower heat and simmer 3 to 5 minutes. Drain shrimp, reserving ½ cup liquid. Peel and devein shrimp; set aside.

Fry bacon in skillet over medium heat; add onion, green pepper, and celery; sauté until onion is golden. Combine flour and cold water; add to skillet mixture and stir until well blended. Add shrimp and cook 3 minutes, stirring constantly. Add ½ cup reserved liquid and hot water; simmer 10 minutes or until thick. Serve over rice, grits, or biscuits. Yield: 4 to 5 servings.
Estelle Walpole,
Johns Island, S.C.

A tempting bowl of Hot Chili (page 68) is one of the easiest and thriftiest ways to please a family.

Overleaf: *Share the festive taste of the holidays with gifts from your kitchen: (clockwise from top left) Orange Tea Bread (page 27), Cranberry-Orange Chutney (page 106), Hot Mocha Mix (page 16), Date Pinwheels (page 79), Glazed Pecans (page 22), Cherry Surprise Balls (page 79), Almond Swirl Ring (page 30), Chocolate Nut Crunch (page 21), Applesauce Fruit-Nut Cake (page 74), Peanut Brittle (page 22), and Baked Country Ham (page 40).*

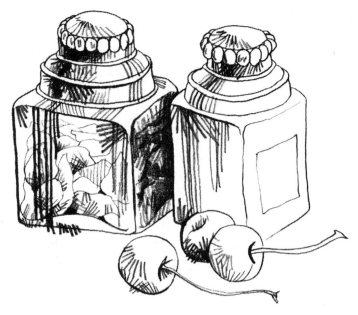

Sweets

With treats like strawberry shortcake, molasses sugar cookies, and old-fashioned apple pie, it's no wonder that Southern custom calls for dessert after every meal.

To honor this tradition, Southern cooks create sweets for every season. We crank up the ice cream freezer to relieve the summer heat, and no Christmas would be complete without the chewy goodness of fruitcake. Days in between give us sweet potato pie and fresh peach cobbler, while anytime is right for homemade brownies. Our specialties will satisfy the sweet tooth of young and old alike.

FRESH APPLE SPICE CAKE

1 cup vegetable oil
2 cups sugar
3 eggs
3 cups all-purpose flour
1 teaspoon soda
¼ teaspoon salt
1 teaspoon ground cinnamon
1 teaspoon ground nutmeg
1 teaspoon vanilla extract
1 cup chopped pecans
3 cups peeled, finely chopped apples
Glaze (recipe follows)

Combine oil and sugar; beat well. Add eggs, one at a time, beating well after each addition. Combine flour, soda, salt, cinnamon, and nutmeg; stir. Add dry ingredients to sugar mixture, beating well. Add vanilla; mix well.

Stir in pecans and apples. Pour batter into a greased and floured 10-inch tube pan. Bake at 350° for 1 hour and 15 minutes or until cake tests done.

Using a toothpick, punch holes in cake while hot; spoon glaze over cake. Cool; remove from pan. Yield: one 10-inch cake.

GLAZE:

½ cup sugar
¼ cup buttermilk
¼ teaspoon soda
2 tablespoons butter or margarine
1½ teaspoons vanilla extract

Combine all ingredients in a medium saucepan. Bring to a boil; boil 4 minutes, stirring occasionally. Yield: about 1 cup.

Betty Giles,
Troutville, Va.

73

APPLE SNACK CAKE

¾ cup vegetable oil
2 eggs
2 cups sugar
2½ cups all-purpose flour
1 teaspoon soda
1 teaspoon baking powder
1 teaspoon salt
1 teaspoon ground cinnamon
3 cups peeled, chopped apples
1 cup chopped pecans
1 (6-ounce) package butterscotch morsels

Combine oil, eggs, and sugar in large mixing bowl; beat at medium speed of electric mixer until well mixed.

Combine flour, soda, baking powder, salt, and cinnamon; stir. Add dry ingredients alternately with apples to egg mixture, mixing well. Stir in pecans and half of butterscotch morsels. Spread batter into a greased 13- x 9- x 2-inch baking pan. Sprinkle batter with remaining morsels. Bake at 350° for 55 to 60 minutes. Yield: about 15 servings.   *Irene Sprinkel, Fincastle, Va.*

APPLESAUCE FRUIT-NUT CAKE

½ cup margarine, softened
1½ cups sugar
2 eggs
1½ cups unsweetened applesauce
2½ cups all-purpose flour, divided
2 teaspoons soda
1 teaspoon baking powder
½ teaspoon salt
1 teaspoon ground cloves
1 teaspoon ground cinnamon
1 teaspoon ground nutmeg
1 cup chopped pecans
1 cup raisins
1 (4-ounce) package candied cherries, chopped
1 (4-ounce) package candied pineapple, chopped
Candied cherries (optional)

Combine margarine and sugar in a large mixing bowl, creaming well. Add eggs, one at a time, mixing well after each addition. Add applesauce, mixing well. (Mixture will appear to be curdled.)

Combine 2 cups flour, soda, baking powder, salt, cloves, cinnamon, and nutmeg; mix well. Gradually add flour mixture to creamed mixture, mixing well.

Combine pecans, raisins, chopped cherries, and pineapple in a large bowl; dredge with remaining ½ cup flour, stirring to coat well. Gently fold mixture into creamed mixture. Spoon batter into a greased and floured 10-inch tube pan. Bake at 325° for 1 hour and 10 minutes or until cake tests done. Cool 10 minutes in pan; remove from pan and complete cooling on wire rack. Garnish with additional candied cherries, if desired. Yield: one 10-inch cake.   *Mrs. Sidney Ingram, Statesville, N.C.*

MILKY WAY CAKE

8 (1-11/16-ounce) chocolate-covered malt-caramel candy bars
½ cup butter or margarine, melted
1½ cups sugar
½ cup butter or margarine, softened
4 eggs, separated
1 teaspoon vanilla extract
1¼ cups buttermilk
½ teaspoon soda
3 cups all-purpose flour
1 cup chopped pecans
Milk Chocolate Frosting

Combine candy bars and ½ cup melted butter in a saucepan; place over low heat until candy bars are melted, stirring constantly. Cool.

Cream sugar and ½ cup softened butter until light and fluffy. Add egg yolks, one at a time, beating well after each addition; stir in vanilla. Combine buttermilk and soda; add to creamed mixture alternately with flour, beating well after each addition. Stir in candy mixture and pecans. Fold in stiffly beaten egg whites.

Pour batter into a greased and floured 10-inch tube pan; bake at 325° for 1 hour and 35 minutes or until done. Let cool in pan 1 hour; remove from pan, and complete cooling on wire rack. Frost with Milk Chocolate Frosting. Yield: one 10-inch cake.

MILK CHOCOLATE FROSTING:

1½ cups sugar
1 cup evaporated milk, undiluted
½ cup butter or margarine, melted
1 (6-ounce) package semisweet chocolate morsels
1 cup marshmallow creme
2 tablespoons milk

Combine sugar, evaporated milk, and butter in a heavy saucepan; cook over medium heat until mixture reaches soft ball stage (237°).

Remove from heat; add chocolate morsels and marshmallow creme, stirring until melted. Add milk and stir until smooth. Yield: frosting for one 10-inch cake. *Opal Moffitt, Duncanville, Ala.*

CREAMY COCONUT CAKE

½ cup shortening
½ cup butter or margarine, softened
2 cups sugar
5 eggs, separated
2 cups all-purpose flour
1 teaspoon soda
¼ teaspoon salt
1 cup buttermilk
1 teaspoon vanilla extract
⅔ cup flaked coconut
Pinch of cream of tartar
Coconut-Pecan Frosting

Cream shortening, butter, and sugar until light and fluffy. Add egg yolks, one at a time, beating well after each addition. Combine flour, soda, and salt; add to creamed mixture alternately with buttermilk, beginning and ending with flour mixture; beat well after each addition. Stir in vanilla and coconut.

Beat egg whites until frothy; add cream of

tartar and continue beating until egg whites are stiff but not dry. Fold egg whites into batter.

Spoon batter into 3 greased and floured 9-inch cakepans. Bake at 350° for 25 to 30 minutes or until cake tests done. Cool thoroughly on wire racks. Spread Coconut-Pecan Frosting between layers and on top and sides of cake. Store in refrigerator. Yield: one 9-inch layer cake.

COCONUT-PECAN FROSTING:

1 (8-ounce) package cream cheese, softened
½ cup butter or margarine, softened
1 (16-ounce) package powdered sugar, sifted
1 teaspoon vanilla extract
Dash of salt
½ cup flaked coconut
½ cup chopped pecans

Beat cream cheese and butter until light and fluffy. Gradually add sugar, beating until smooth. Add vanilla and salt; beat until thoroughly blended. Stir in coconut and pecans. Yield: enough for one 3-layer cake. *Mrs. Leonard G. Voegeli, Amber, Okla.*

SOUTHERN GINGERBREAD

3 cups all-purpose flour
2 teaspoons ground ginger
1 teaspoon soda
1 teaspoon salt
1½ cups molasses
½ cup boiling water
¼ cup butter or margarine, melted
Whipped cream

Combine dry ingredients; stir well. Combine molasses, water, and butter, mixing well. Add molasses mixture to dry ingredients, stirring until smooth. Pour into a greased 9-inch square baking pan; bake at 350° for 30 to 40 minutes. Cut into 3-inch squares. Serve warm with whipped cream. Yield: 9 servings. *Clara Paysinger, Salem, Ark.*

LEMON MOIST CUPCAKES

¾ cup butter or margarine, softened
1 cup sugar
2 eggs
2 cups self-rising flour
½ cup milk
1 teaspoon vanilla extract
1 cup sugar
Grated rind of 1 lemon
Grated rind of 1 orange
Juice of 2 lemons
Juice of 2 oranges

Combine butter and 1 cup sugar in a large mixing bowl, creaming until light and fluffy. Add eggs, beating well. Stir in flour. Add milk and vanilla, mixing just until blended.

Spoon batter into paper-lined muffin tins, filling each cup half full. Bake at 350° for 20 to 25 minutes or until they test done.

Combine remaining ingredients in a small mixing bowl, stirring until blended. Spoon glaze over warm cupcakes. Yield: about 2 dozen.
Mrs. Lyman Clayborn,
Kinston, N.C.

FAVORITE HOLIDAY CAKE

1 cup shortening
2 cups sugar
5 eggs
1 cup all-purpose flour
1 cup self-rising flour
1 cup milk
2 teaspoons vanilla extract
Coconut Filling
Chocolate Frosting

Cream shortening; gradually add sugar, beating until light and fluffy and sugar is dissolved. Add eggs, one at a time, beating well after each addition.

Combine flour; add to creamed mixture alternately with milk, beginning and ending with flour mixture. Add vanilla, mixing well.

Pour into 2 greased and floured 9-inch cakepans. Bake at 350° for 30 to 35 minutes or until cake tests done. Cool in pans 10 minutes; remove from pans and cool completely.

Split cake layers in half horizontally. Place half of one cake layer, cut side up, on a cake plate; spread evenly with one-third of Coconut Filling. Repeat procedure with second and third layers. Place remaining layer, cut side down, on top of cake. Frost with Chocolate Frosting. Yield: one 9-inch layer cake.

COCONUT FILLING:

1 cup sugar
1 cup milk
1 pound frozen coconut
12 large marshmallows
1 teaspoon vanilla extract

Combine sugar and milk in a saucepan; bring to a boil. Add coconut and marshmallows; boil over medium heat for 5 minutes. Remove from heat; stir in vanilla. Yield: 2½ cups.

CHOCOLATE FROSTING:

2 cups sugar
½ cup butter or margarine
1 cup evaporated milk
2 to 3 tablespoons cocoa

Combine all ingredients; cook over medium heat almost to soft ball stage (230°), stirring constantly. Remove from heat. Beat until thick enough to spread. Yield: enough frosting for one 9-inch layer cake. *Mrs. Bobby Norris,*
Guin, Ala.

KENTUCKY PECAN CAKE

2½ cups self-rising flour
2 cups sugar
1½ cups vegetable oil
1 cup applesauce
2½ tablespoons ground cinnamon
4 egg yolks
2 tablespoons hot water
1 cup chopped pecans
4 egg whites

Combine first 7 ingredients in order listed; beat until smooth. Stir in pecans.

Beat egg whites until stiff; fold into batter. Pour mixture into an ungreased 10-inch tube pan. Bake at 350° for 1 hour and 30 minutes. Invert pan and cool cake completely; remove from pan. Yield: one 10-inch cake.

Sherlon Page,
Spring Hope, N.C.

ORANGE SLICE CAKE

3½ cups all-purpose flour
½ teaspoon salt
1 pound candy orange slices, chopped
1 (8-ounce) package chopped dates
2 cups chopped pecans
1 (3½-ounce) can flaked coconut
¾ cup butter or margarine, softened
2 cups sugar
4 eggs
½ cup buttermilk
1 teaspoon soda
½ cup orange juice
½ cup sifted powdered sugar

Combine flour and salt; stir and set aside.

Combine orange slices, dates, pecans, and coconut; stir in ½ cup flour mixture. Set aside.

Cream butter; gradually add sugar, beating until light and fluffy and sugar is dissolved. Add eggs, one at a time, beating well after each addition.

Combine buttermilk and soda, mixing well. Add flour mixture alternately with buttermilk to creamed mixture, beginning and ending with flour. Add candy mixture; stir until well blended.

Spoon batter into a greased and floured 10-inch tube pan. Bake at 300° for 2 hours or until cake tests done.

Combine orange juice and powdered sugar. Punch holes in top of cake using a toothpick. Spoon glaze over cake while still hot. Remove cake from pan when cool. Yield: one 10-inch cake.   *Mrs. Raymond Lunsford,*
Hilton, Va.

FRUITED POUND CAKE

1 cup butter, softened
1 (8-ounce) package cream cheese, softened
1½ cups sugar
4 eggs
2¼ cups all-purpose flour, divided
1½ teaspoons baking powder
Grated rind of 1 lemon
1 cup chopped mixed candied fruit
½ cup golden seedless raisins
½ cup dates, chopped
½ cup chopped pecans
Candied cherries (optional)
Candied pineapple slices (optional)
Powdered sugar

Cream butter and cream cheese; gradually add sugar, beating until light and fluffy and sugar is dissolved. Add eggs, one at a time, beating well after each addition.

Combine 1¾ cups flour and baking powder; gradually add to creamed mixture and beat until well blended.

Dredge lemon rind, candied fruit, raisins, dates, and pecans with remaining ½ cup flour; stir to coat well. Stir mixture into batter.

Spoon into a greased and floured 10-inch tube pan. Bake at 325° for 1 hour and 20 minutes or until done. Cool cake about 10 minutes before removing from pan. Garnish with candied cherries and pineapple, if desired. Dust top of cake with powdered sugar. Yield: one 10-inch cake.   *Mrs. Elaine Bell,*
Dexter, N. Mex.

Tip: For a successful cake, measure ingredients accurately, follow recipe without making substitutions, and use size pans recommended.

When baking a layer cake, don't let pans touch each other or sides of oven; stagger their placement so that heat circulates evenly.

To test cake for doneness, touch lightly in center. Cake will spring back if it is done. It should also pull away from sides of pan.

STRAWBERRY SHORTCAKE

4 cups fresh strawberries, sliced
4 to 6 tablespoons sugar
2 cups biscuit mix
2 tablespoons sugar
⅔ cup half-and-half
¼ cup butter or margarine, melted
1 egg, beaten
Sweetened whipped cream or frozen whipped
    topping, thawed

Combine strawberries and 4 to 6 table-spoons sugar; chill. Combine biscuit mix, sugar, half-and-half, butter, and egg; beat at high speed of electric mixer 30 seconds. Spoon batter into a greased 8-inch cakepan. Bake at 425° for 15 to 20 minutes or until golden brown. Turn out onto wire rack to cool.

Slice shortcake crosswise into 2 equal parts. Place bottom half of shortcake cut side up on a serving dish; spoon half of strawberries on bottom layer. Top with second layer of short-cake, cut side down; spoon on remaining straw-berries. Top with whipped cream. Cut into wedges to serve. Yield: 6 to 8 servings.

Note: 4 cups sliced fresh peaches may be substituted for strawberries.

Mrs. Debra Lancaster,
Hawkinsville, Ga.

SWEET POTATO CAKE SQUARES

½ cup shortening
2 cups sugar
1 cup cooked, mashed sweet potatoes
1 teaspoon vanilla extract
4 eggs
1½ cups self-rising flour
1 teaspoon ground cinnamon
1 teaspoon ground nutmeg

Cream shortening and sugar; add sweet potatoes and vanilla, mixing well. Add eggs, one at a time, mixing well after each addition.

Combine flour, cinnamon, and nutmeg;

add to sweet potato mixture; mix well. Pour into a greased 13- x 9- x 2-inch baking pan. Bake at 300° for 1 hour or until cake tests done. Yield: 15 servings.   *Mrs. Kenneth Tubbs,*
Oak Grove, La.

CHEWY FUDGE BROWNIES

1 cup shortening
3 cups sugar
6 eggs, slightly beaten
6 (1-ounce) squares unsweetened chocolate,
    melted
2 cups all-purpose flour
1 teaspoon baking powder
1 teaspoon salt
2 teaspoons vanilla extract
1 cup chopped pecans or walnuts

Combine shortening, sugar, and eggs; mix until blended. Add chocolate and mix well. Combine dry ingredients; add to chocolate mix-ture, mixing well. Stir in vanilla and nuts. Spread in a greased and floured 15- x 10- x 1-inch jellyroll pan. Bake at 350° for 30 to 35 minutes. Cool and cut into bars. Yield: about 2½ dozen.   *Nina Ward,*
Caldwell, Kans.

CARROT-ORANGE COOKIES

¾ cup shortening
¾ cup sugar
1 cup cooked mashed carrots
1 egg
1 teaspoon vanilla extract
¾ teaspoon orange extract
2 cups all-purpose flour
2 teaspoons baking powder
½ teaspoon salt
½ cup raisins
¼ cup chopped nuts

Cream shortening and sugar until light and fluffy; add next 4 ingredients, beating well.

Combine flour, baking powder, and salt; gradually add to creamed mixture. Stir in raisins and nuts. Drop by rounded teaspoonfuls onto greased cookie sheets. Bake at 350° for 12 to 15 minutes. Yield: about 5½ dozen.

Gail Marshall,
Camden, Tenn.

CHERRY SURPRISE BALLS

1 cup butter or margarine, softened
½ cup powdered sugar
2 cups all-purpose flour
1 teaspoon vanilla extract
½ cup chopped pecans
1 pound red candied cherries
Powdered sugar

Combine butter and ½ cup powdered sugar; cream until light and fluffy. Add flour and vanilla, mixing well; stir in pecans. Wrap dough in waxed paper and chill 2 to 3 hours.

Cover each cherry with enough dough to make a ¾-inch ball. Place on ungreased cookie sheets and chill 15 minutes. Bake at 375° for 18 to 20 minutes; let cool slightly and roll in powdered sugar. Yield: about 6½ dozen.

Kitti Cromer,
Anderson, S.C.

DATE PINWHEELS

1 cup shortening
2 cups firmly packed brown sugar
3 eggs
4¼ cups all-purpose flour
1 teaspoon salt
1 teaspoon soda
1 teaspoon baking powder
1 teaspoon ground cinnamon
Date Filling

Combine shortening and sugar; cream until light and fluffy. Add eggs and beat well. Combine next 5 ingredients; gradually add to creamed mixture, mixing well. Shape dough into a ball; chill dough 3 to 4 hours.

Divide dough into 3 equal parts; roll each part into a 14- x 10-inch rectangle on waxed paper. Spread one-third of Date Filling over dough on each rectangle, leaving a 1-inch margin on all sides. Starting at long end, carefully roll dough, jellyroll fashion; pinch lengthwise seam and ends of roll to seal. Cover and refrigerate several hours or overnight.

Slice dough into ½-inch-thick slices. Place on ungreased cookie sheets, 1 inch apart. Bake at 350° for 15 minutes. Yield: about 7½ dozen.

DATE FILLING:

2 (8-ounce) packages dates, pitted and chopped
½ cup sugar
⅔ cup water
1 cup chopped pecans or walnuts

Combine dates, sugar, and water in a medium saucepan; mix well. Cook over medium heat about 10 minutes or until thickened, stirring constantly. Remove from heat; stir in pecans. Let cool. Yield: about 2½ cups.

Mrs. Jerry Rusert,
Mena, Ark.

MOLASSES SUGAR COOKIES

¾ cup shortening
1 cup sugar
¼ cup molasses
1 egg, beaten
2¼ cups all-purpose flour
2 teaspoons soda
½ teaspoon salt
½ teaspoon ground cloves
1 teaspoon ground ginger
1 teaspoon ground cinnamon
Sugar

Melt shortening and cool. Add 1 cup sugar, molasses, and egg; mix well. Combine flour, soda, salt, and spices; add to sugar mixture, mixing until blended. Shape into 1-inch balls; roll in sugar. Place 2 inches apart on greased cookie sheets; bake at 375° for 8 minutes or until done. Yield: about 4 dozen.

Mrs. Edgar Patterson,
Carrollton, Ga.

BIG MAMA'S PEACH SQUARES

2 cups all-purpose flour
½ cup powdered sugar
⅛ teaspoon salt
1 cup butter or margarine, softened
4 eggs, slightly beaten
2 ripe peaches, pureed
2 cups sugar
½ cup cornstarch
Powdered sugar

Combine flour, powdered sugar, and salt in bowl; cut in butter until well blended. Press dough evenly into a 15- x 10- x 1-inch jellyroll pan. Bake at 350° for 15 to 20 minutes.

Combine next 4 ingredients; mix well. Pour peach mixture over hot crust; bake at 350° for 25 minutes. Cut into 3- x 2-inch bars when cool. Dust with powdered sugar. Yield: 25 bars.

Georgia Grunewald,
Girard, Ga.

CRINKLE SUNFLOWER COOKIES

¾ cup shortening
1 cup sugar
1 cup firmly packed light brown sugar
2 eggs, slightly beaten
1 teaspoon vanilla extract
2 cups all-purpose flour
½ teaspoon baking powder
1 teaspoon soda
¼ teaspoon salt
2 cups regular oats, uncooked
1 cup flaked coconut
1 (4-ounce) package salted sunflower seeds

Combine shortening and sugar, creaming well; beat in eggs and vanilla. Add dry ingredients; mix well. Add remaining ingredients, stirring until blended. Drop by rounded teaspoonfuls onto greased cookie sheets; bake at 350° for 13 to 15 minutes or until edges begin to brown. Yield: about 9½ dozen.

Mrs. John Evanson,
Judsonia, Ark.

PEANUT BUTTER FROSTS

1 cup all-purpose flour
1 cup quick-cooking oats
½ cup sugar
½ cup firmly packed brown sugar
½ teaspoon soda
½ cup butter or margarine, softened
⅓ cup peanut butter
1 egg, beaten
Peanut Butter Frosting
Chopped peanuts (optional)

Combine flour, oats, sugar, and soda in a large bowl. Add butter, peanut butter, and egg; stir until thoroughly blended. (Mixture will be crumbly.) Press in a greased 9-inch square pan. Bake at 350° for 20 to 25 minutes or until the edges begin to pull away from sides of pan. (The center will be soft.) Cool completely. Top with Peanut Butter Frosting. Sprinkle with chopped peanuts, if desired. Cut into 3- x 1½-inch bars. Yield: 1½ dozen.

PEANUT BUTTER FROSTING:

¼ cup butter or margarine, softened
1½ cups powdered sugar, divided
¼ cup peanut butter
1 tablespoon plus 2 teaspoons milk
1 teaspoon vanilla extract

Combine butter and 1 cup sugar in a small mixing bowl; beat until creamy. Add remaining ½ cup sugar, peanut butter, milk, and vanilla; beat until fluffy. Add additional milk if needed for smooth consistency. Yield: about 1¼ cups.

Mrs. Galen Johnson,
Transylvania, La.

BUTTER PECAN COOKIES

2 cups all-purpose flour
½ teaspoon salt
1 cup butter, softened
2 tablespoons sugar
¼ cup light molasses
2 cups finely chopped pecans
Powdered sugar

Combine flour and salt; set aside.

Cream butter and sugar in a large mixing bowl until light and fluffy. Add molasses; mix until well blended. Gradually add flour mixture to butter mixture; mix well. Stir in nuts.

Roll dough into 1-inch balls; place about 2 inches apart on ungreased cookie sheets. Bake at 350° for 15 to 18 minutes. Dust or roll warm cookies in powdered sugar. Yield: about 5 dozen. *Varniece R. Warren,*
Hermitage, Ark.

CHERRY ICE CREAM

8 eggs
2½ cups sugar
½ teaspoon salt
3 (13-ounce) cans evaporated milk, chilled
2 (21-ounce) cans cherry pie filling
3¾ cups milk

Using high speed of electric mixer, beat eggs 3 minutes in a large mixing bowl; gradually add sugar and salt, continuing to beat. Add evaporated milk and pie filling, mixing until combined. Stir in milk.

Pour mixture into freezer can of a 1½-gallon hand-turned or electric freezer. Freeze according to manufacturer's instructions. Let ripen at least 1½ hours. Yield: 1½ gallons.

Note: To freeze in a 1-gallon freezer, divide mixture and freeze each half separately. Refrigerate mixture until freezing. *Mary Alice Curl,*
Miami, Tex.

Tip: Use shiny cookie sheets rather than darkened ones. Dark pans absorb more heat and can cause baked products to overbrown.

HOMEMADE STRAWBERRY ICE CREAM

1 (5½-ounce) package vanilla instant pudding and pie filling mix
2 cups sugar
4 cups milk
1 cup water
1 (13-ounce) can evaporated milk
2 cups mashed fresh strawberries (or other fresh fruit)

Combine dry ingredients in a large bowl; add remaining ingredients, stirring to mix. Pour mixture into freezer can of a 1-gallon hand-turned or electric freezer. Freeze according to manufacturer's instructions. Let ripen at least 1 hour. Yield: 1 gallon. *Nancy Monroe,*
Elizabethtown, N.C.

VANILLA ICE CREAM SPECTACULAR

5 cups milk
2¼ cups sugar
6 tablespoons all-purpose flour
½ teaspoon salt
5 eggs, beaten
1 quart whipping cream
1 tablespoon plus 1½ teaspoons vanilla extract

Heat milk in a saucepan over low heat until scalded. Combine sugar, flour, and salt in a 3-quart saucepan; gradually stir in milk. Cook over medium heat for 15 minutes or until thickened, stirring constantly.

Stir some of hot mixture into beaten eggs; add to remaining hot mixture, stirring constantly. Cook 1 minute; remove from heat and cool. Chill 1½ to 2 hours.

Combine cream and vanilla in a large bowl; add chilled custard, stirring with a wire whisk to combine. Pour mixture into freezer can of a 1-gallon hand-turned or electric freezer. Freeze according to manufacturer's instructions. Let ripen 1½ to 2 hours. Yield: 1 gallon.

Dorothy L. Anderson,
Manor, Tex.

BUTTERMILK SHERBET

2 cups buttermilk
1 cup sugar
1 (8-ounce) can crushed pineapple, undrained
1 tablespoon vanilla extract
2 egg whites

Combine buttermilk, sugar, pineapple, and vanilla, mixing well. Place in an airtight container and freeze mixture until slushy.

Beat egg whites until stiff but not dry. Add buttermilk mixture and beat well. Pour into airtight freezer container and freeze until firm. Yield: about 1 quart. *Pertie Bickley, Louisa, Va.*

BLUEBERRY YUM-YUM

2 cups fresh blueberries
2 cups sugar, divided
¼ cup water
¼ cup cornstarch
3 tablespoons water
1 cup all-purpose flour
½ cup margarine, softened
1 cup finely chopped pecans
1 (8-ounce) package cream cheese, softened
1 (9-ounce) container frozen whipped topping, thawed

Combine blueberries, 1 cup sugar, and ¼ cup water in a medium saucepan; cook over low heat until berries are soft (about 15 minutes). Combine cornstarch and 3 tablespoons water in a small mixing bowl; stir well. Add cornstarch mixture to blueberry mixture; cook, stirring constantly, until thickened. Set aside to cool.

Combine flour, margarine, and pecans in a small mixing bowl; mix well. Press dough evenly into a 13- x 9- x 2-inch baking dish. Bake at 350° for 20 minutes; cool.

Combine cream cheese and 1 cup sugar; beat until smooth. Fold in whipped topping. Spread topping evenly over cooled crust. Pour blueberry mixture evenly over top. Refrigerate; cut into squares to serve. Yield: 15 servings. *Audrey Shelton, Altha, Fla.*

EASY PEACHY DESSERT

½ cup butter or margarine
¾ cup chopped pecans
1½ cups crushed corn-flavored cereal squares
½ cup firmly packed brown sugar
Pinch of ground nutmeg
3 cups sliced, cooked peaches
1 (8-ounce) carton frozen whipped topping, thawed
1 (3¾-ounce) package vanilla instant pudding and pie filling mix

Melt butter in heavy skillet. Add pecans; cook over medium heat, stirring constantly, 3 to 5 minutes or until toasted. Stir in cereal crumbs, brown sugar, and nutmeg.

Press half of crumb mixture into an 8-inch square baking pan. Put pan into freezer for 15 minutes.

Combine peaches, whipped topping, and pudding mix; gently stir to mix. Spoon peach mixture over crumb mixture; spread evenly. Sprinkle remaining crumb mixture over peach mixture. Place dessert in freezer 2 hours. Yield: 9 servings. *Marguerite Alley, Girard, Ga.*

RASPBERRY RHAPSODY

1⅓ cups all-purpose flour
3 tablespoons sugar
¾ cup margarine, softened
⅓ cup chopped pecans
1 (8-ounce) package cream cheese, softened
⅔ cup sugar
1 (12-ounce) carton frozen whipped topping, thawed and divided
2 (3¾-ounce) packages French vanilla instant pudding and pie filling mix
1½ cups milk
1 (10-ounce) package raspberries, thawed and drained
Fresh raspberries (optional)

Combine flour and 3 tablespoons sugar in a small mixing bowl; cut in margarine with pastry blender until mixture resembles coarse meal.

Stir in pecans. Press pecan mixture into a 13- x 9- x 2-inch baking dish. Bake at 350° for 15 minutes; cool completely.

Combine cream cheese and ⅔ cup sugar; beat until smooth. Add half of whipped topping; beat until blended. Spread over cooled crust; chill.

Combine pudding mix and milk; beat 2 minutes at medium speed of electric mixer. Fold in thawed raspberries. Spread pudding mixture over cream cheese layer. Spread remaining whipped topping over pudding layer. Garnish with fresh raspberries, if desired. Chill until serving time. Cut into squares to serve. Yield: 18 servings. *Lois Ballard, Knoxville, Tenn.*

and beat until fluffy. Spread topping over strawberry filling. Chill several hours; cut into squares. Top each serving with a whole strawberry, if desired. Yield: 9 servings.

Mrs. Artie B. Lowe, Milledgeville, Ga.

STRAWBERRY-CREAM CHEESE DESSERT

1½ cups graham cracker crumbs
½ cup butter or margarine, melted
3 tablespoons sugar
½ cup chopped pecans
½ cup chopped almonds
1 (3-ounce) package strawberry-flavored gelatin
1 pint fresh strawberries
1 (8-ounce) package cream cheese, softened
3 tablespoons powdered sugar
1 (1.5-ounce) package whipped topping mix
9 whole fresh strawberries (optional)

Combine graham cracker crumbs, butter, sugar, and nuts; stir well. Press crumb mixture into an 8-inch square pan. Bake at 350° for 8 to 10 minutes or until light brown. Cool on wire rack.

Prepare gelatin according to package directions; chill until it reaches consistency of unbeaten egg white. Remove stems from 1 pint strawberries; rinse and drain. Slice strawberries and stir into gelatin. Spoon gelatin mixture into crust; chill until firm.

Combine cream cheese and powdered sugar; beat until light and fluffy.

Prepare whipped topping mix according to package directions; add cream cheese mixture

STRAWBERRY DESSERT

¼ cup firmly packed brown sugar
½ cup butter or margarine, softened
1 cup all-purpose flour
¾ cup chopped pecans
⅔ cup milk
30 large marshmallows
1 (1.5-ounce) package whipped topping mix
1 (3-ounce) package strawberry-flavored gelatin
1 cup boiling water
¾ cup cold water
2 cups fresh strawberries, sliced

Cream brown sugar and butter until smooth. Add flour and stir until mixture resembles coarse crumbs. Add pecans. Press into a 13- x 9- x 2-inch pan. Bake at 350° for 15 minutes; cool.

Combine milk and marshmallows; stir over low heat until marshmallows melt. Prepare whipped topping mix according to package directions and fold into marshmallow mixture. Pour over crumb crust and chill. Dissolve gelatin in boiling water; stir in cold water. Chill until it reaches consistency of unbeaten egg white. Fold in sliced strawberries; pour over marshmallow layer. Chill until firm. Yield: 10 to 12 servings. *Mrs. Galen Johnson, Transylvania, La.*

Fruits and Puddings 83

ORANGE PUDDING

2 eggs, separated
½ cup sugar, divided
¼ teaspoon salt
2 tablespoons all-purpose flour
2 tablespoons butter or margarine, softened
1 tablespoon grated orange rind
¼ cup fresh orange juice
1 tablespoon fresh lemon juice
1 cup milk

Beat egg whites until frothy; add ¼ cup sugar and salt; continue beating until soft peaks form. Set aside.

Beat egg yolks until lemon colored; add flour, butter, orange rind, juice, and remaining sugar. Gradually beat in milk. Fold egg white mixture into pudding. Spoon into 6 (6-ounce) buttered custard cups. Place in a pan of hot water; bake at 350° for 35 to 40 minutes or until a knife inserted in center comes out clean. Chill. Yield: 6 servings.   *Varniece Warren,*
Hermitage, Ark.

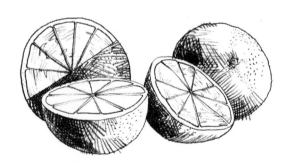

BLUEBERRY SYRUP

4 cups fresh blueberries
1 cup water
½ cup sugar
2 tablespoons cornstarch

Combine all ingredients in a medium saucepan; mix well. Cook over medium heat, stirring constantly, until thickened and bubbly. Serve warm over ice cream, pancakes, or waffles. Yield: about 4 cups.

Maudie Malcolm,
Tifton, Ga.

DELUXE PIE CRUST

2½ cups graham cracker crumbs
2 tablespoons light brown sugar
¼ cup ground pecans
½ cup margarine, softened

Combine graham cracker crumbs, sugar, and pecans; stir in margarine, and mix well. Press mixture firmly and evenly into a 9-inch pieplate. Bake at 350° for 12 to 15 minutes. Yield: one 9-inch pie shell.

OATMEAL PIE CRUST

1 cup all-purpose flour
1 teaspoon salt
¼ cup sugar
½ cup shortening or lard
½ cup regular oats, uncooked
3 to 4 tablespoons water

Combine flour, salt, and sugar in a mixing bowl; cut in shortening until mixture resembles coarse meal. Stir in oats. Sprinkle water evenly over surface; stir with a fork until all ingredients are moistened.

Shape dough into a ball; chill. Roll to fit a 9-inch piepan. Yield: one 9-inch pastry shell.

NEVER FAIL PASTRY

4 cups all-purpose flour
1 teaspoon baking powder
1 teaspoon salt
1 tablespoon sugar
1¾ cups shortening
1 egg, beaten
1 tablespoon vinegar
½ cup cold water

Combine dry ingredients; cut in shortening until mixture resembles coarse meal. Stir in remaining ingredients. Divide dough into 5 equal parts; shape each into a ball and wrap tightly. Chill. May be stored up to 2 weeks in refrigerator. Yield: pastry for five 9-inch pies.

APPLE CRUMB PIE

4 medium or 3 large cooking apples, peeled,
    cored, and thinly sliced
1 unbaked 9-inch pastry shell
1 teaspoon ground cinnamon
1 cup sugar, divided
¾ cup all-purpose flour
⅓ cup butter

Arrange apple slices evenly in pastry shell.
Combine cinnamon and ½ cup sugar; stir well,
and sprinkle mixture over apples.

Combine flour and remaining sugar; stir
well. Cut butter into flour mixture with a pastry
blender until mixture resembles coarse meal.
Sprinkle over apples. Bake at 400° for 40 to 50
minutes. Yield: one 9-inch pie.   *Nina Ward,*
Caldwell, Kans.

DEEP-DISH APPLE PIE

8 cooking apples, peeled and thinly sliced
1¼ cups sugar
3 tablespoons all-purpose flour
1½ teaspoons ground cinnamon
¼ teaspoon ground nutmeg
⅛ teaspoon salt
3 tablespoons butter or margarine
Pastry (recipe follows)

Arrange apple slices in a lightly greased
9-inch square baking dish. Combine sugar,
flour, cinnamon, nutmeg, and salt; sprinkle
over apples, and dot with butter. Top with
pastry, and bake at 400° for 40 minutes or until
golden brown. Yield: 6 to 8 servings.

PASTRY:

1¼ cups all-purpose flour
¼ teaspoon salt
2 tablespoons shortening
¼ cup cold butter or margarine
3 to 4 tablespoons cold water

Combine flour and salt; cut in shortening.
Cut butter into small pieces, and add to flour
mixture; cut in until mixture resembles coarse
meal. Stir in only enough water to moisten

flour; form dough into a ball. Wrap in plastic
wrap, and chill 30 minutes.

Roll dough to ¼-inch thickness on a lightly
floured surface, and cut into 1-inch-wide strips.
Arrange lattice fashion over filling. Yield:
pastry for one 9-inch pie.   *Elaine Gunter,*
Newport, Tenn.

SOUR CREAM APPLE PIE

¾ cup sugar
2 tablespoons all-purpose flour
1 cup commercial sour cream
1 egg, beaten
½ teaspoon vanilla extract
Dash of salt
2 cups peeled, chopped apples
1 unbaked 9-inch pastry shell
Topping (recipe follows)

Combine first 6 ingredients; stir well. Add
apples and spoon into pastry shell. Bake at 375°
for 15 minutes. Reduce heat to 325° and bake
for 15 minutes. Sprinkle topping over pie; continue baking at 325° for 15 minutes. Yield: one
9-inch pie.

TOPPING:

⅓ cup all-purpose flour
⅓ cup firmly packed brown sugar
¼ cup butter or margarine, melted
1 teaspoon ground cinnamon

Combine all ingredients; mix well. Yield:
about ¾ cup.   *Nora Sprinkle,*
Troutville, Va.

*Tip: If baked foods consistently undercook or
overcook at the temperatures and cooking times
specified in recipes, have the thermostat of your
oven checked. Home service advisors of the gas
or electric company will usually do this for you.
However, you can check it yourself with a de-
pendable oven thermometer. Place the thermometer in the center of the oven, and set the oven on
the desired temperature. Allow enough time for
the oven to heat, and compare the thermometer
reading with the oven setting.*

BLUEBERRY DUMPLINGS

4 cups fresh blueberries, divided
½ cup sugar
2 tablespoons all-purpose flour
¼ teaspoon ground cinnamon
⅓ cup sugar
⅓ cup water
Pastry for double-crust 9-inch pie
6 tablespoons butter or margarine
⅓ cup sugar

Combine 2 cups blueberries, ½ cup sugar, flour, and cinnamon in a medium mixing bowl; stir well and set aside. Combine 2 cups blueberries, ⅓ cup sugar, and water in a medium saucepan; bring to a boil. Reduce heat; simmer until berries are soft (about 15 minutes). Press soft berries through a sieve, reserving 1 cup juice; set aside.

Roll out pastry on a floured surface to an 18- x 12-inch rectangle; cut into 6-inch squares. Place ⅓ cup blueberry mixture in center of each square; place 1 tablespoon butter on top of each. Moisten edges of dumplings with water; bring corners to center, pinching edges to seal.

Place dumplings in a greased 13- x 9- x 2-inch baking pan and pour blueberry juice over them. Sprinkle ⅓ cup sugar over top. Bake at 375° for 35 minutes. Serve dumplings warm. Yield: 6 servings. *Hazel Wimer, Hightown, Va.*

BLUEBERRY PIE

2½ cups fresh blueberries, divided
1 baked 9-inch pastry shell
1 cup sugar
3 tablespoons cornstarch
¼ cup water
1 tablespoon margarine
1 teaspoon vanilla extract
1 (4-ounce) container frozen whipped topping, thawed

Pour 1¼ cups blueberries into pastry shell; spread evenly, and set aside. Combine 1 cup blueberries, sugar, cornstarch, and water in a

medium saucepan; cook and stir over low heat until thickened. Remove from heat; stir in margarine and vanilla; cool. Pour over blueberries in pastry shell. Chill. Spoon whipped topping around edge; garnish with ¼ cup blueberries. Yield: one 9-inch pie. *E. Gayle Pace, Raleigh, N.C.*

EGG CUSTARD PIE

4 eggs, well beaten
2 cups milk
1 cup sugar
1 teaspoon vanilla extract
Pinch of salt
1 unbaked 9-inch pastry shell

Combine eggs, milk, sugar, vanilla, and salt; mix well. Pour into pastry shell; bake at 425° for 35 to 40 minutes or until a knife inserted halfway between center and edge comes out clean. Serve slightly warm or cold. Yield: one 9-inch pie.

Note: The center of pie may not be firm when pie is removed from oven, but it will firm up when cooled. Overbaking will make custard watery. *Ozema Kelley, Eldridge, Ala.*

CHOCOLATE MERINGUE PIE

3 cups sifted all-purpose flour
1 cup shortening
6 tablespoons ice water
1 egg, well beaten
2 cups milk
1 cup sugar
¼ cup plus 2 tablespoons all-purpose flour
¼ cup plus 2 tablespoons cocoa
¼ teaspoon salt
3 egg yolks, slightly beaten
1 tablespoon butter or margarine
1 teaspoon vanilla extract
Meringue (recipe follows)

Place 3 cups flour in a bowl; cut in shortening until mixture resembles coarse meal. Add water and egg; stir with a fork until all dry ingredients are moistened. Shape dough into a ball; roll out to fit a 9-inch piepan. Bake at 450° for 10 to 12 minutes or until golden brown. Cool. (Shape leftover dough into a ball; wrap and store in refrigerator. It can be stored for up to one week.)

Place milk in a double boiler; combine dry ingredients and add to milk. Cook until thickened, stirring constantly. Stir about one-fourth of hot mixture into egg yolks; add to remaining hot mixture and cook 2 or 3 minutes, stirring constantly. Remove from heat; add butter and vanilla. Beat with mixer for 2 to 3 minutes; cool.

Pour filling into pastry shell. Top with meringue. Bake at 350° for 12 minutes or until lightly browned. Yield: one 9-inch pie.

MERINGUE:

3 egg whites
¼ teaspoon cream of tartar
¼ cup plus 2 tablespoons sugar

Combine egg whites and cream of tartar; beat until foamy. Gradually add sugar, beating until stiff. Yield: enough for one 9-inch pie.
Nellie Kate Tepper,
Selma, Ala.

LIME FLUFF PIE

1 (3-ounce) package lime-flavored gelatin
1 cup boiling water
¼ cup sugar
¼ cup frozen limeade concentrate, thawed and undiluted
⅓ cup cold water
1 (8-ounce) package cream cheese, softened
1 (1.5-ounce) envelope whipped topping mix
Crispy Rice Crust

Combine gelatin, boiling water, and sugar; stir until dissolved. Stir in limeade concentrate and cold water; set aside.

Beat cream cheese until smooth in a large mixing bowl. Add ¼ cup gelatin mixture, one tablespoon at a time, beating after each addi-

tion. Gradually add remaining gelatin mixture, beating until smooth. Chill 1 hour and 15 minutes or until thickened, stirring occasionally.

Prepare whipped topping mix according to package directions, omitting vanilla; fold into thickened gelatin mixture. Chill 45 minutes or until mixture mounds.

Pour filling into Crispy Rice Crust. Chill at least 3 hours. Yield: one 9-inch pie.

CRISPY RICE CRUST:

4 cups bite-size crispy rice squares cereal, crushed (will make 1¼ cups)
¼ cup firmly packed brown sugar
6 tablespoons melted butter or margarine

Combine cereal crumbs and sugar in a small mixing bowl. Stir in butter; combine well. Press mixture evenly into a 9-inch piepan. Bake at 300° for 10 minutes; cool. Yield: one 9-inch pie shell.
Varniece R. Warren,
Hermitage, Ark.

MINIATURE PECAN PIES

½ cup sugar
1 cup dark corn syrup
1 tablespoon butter or margarine
¼ teaspoon salt
3 eggs
1 cup coarsely chopped pecans
½ teaspoon vanilla extract
16 (2-inch) unbaked tart shells

Combine sugar, syrup, butter, and salt in a saucepan. Bring mixture to a boil, stirring constantly; remove from heat.

Crack eggs in a medium bowl; remove 1 tablespoon egg white and set aside. Beat remaining eggs with a fork until well combined. Gradually stir hot mixture into beaten eggs. Add pecans and vanilla; stir until combined.

Beat reserved egg white until foamy; brush inside of tart shells lightly with beaten egg white. Fill tart shells three-fourths full with filling. Bake at 450° for 5 minutes; reduce heat to 325° and bake 12 minutes or until set. Yield: 16 (2-inch) pies.

SPECIAL PECAN PIE

½ cup sugar
2 tablespoons all-purpose flour
1 cup dark corn syrup
2 eggs
3 tablespoons margarine, softened
½ teaspoon vanilla extract
1½ cups chopped pecans
1 unbaked 9-inch pastry shell

Combine sugar and flour; add corn syrup, eggs, and margarine. Beat well; stir in vanilla and pecans. Pour into pastry shell. Bake at 325° for 1 hour or until firm. Yield: one 9-inch pie.
Louise Floyd,
Selma, Ala.

SWEET POTATO CREAM PIE IN GINGERSNAP CRUST

¾ cup evaporated milk
¾ cup water
1½ cups cooked, mashed sweet potatoes
½ cup dark corn syrup
⅓ cup sugar
3 tablespoons cornstarch
1 teaspoon ground cinnamon
¾ teaspoon ground ginger
½ teaspoon salt
2 eggs, well beaten
½ teaspoon vanilla extract
3 tablespoons butter or margarine
Gingersnap Crust
Sweetened whipped cream (optional)
Chopped pecans (optional)

Combine milk and water in a large saucepan; scald. Add sweet potatoes and syrup; mix well. Combine sugar, cornstarch, cinnamon, ginger, and salt; mix well. Gradually add sugar mixture to milk mixture, stirring until thickened. Stir about one-fourth of hot mixture into eggs; add to remaining hot mixture, stirring constantly. Cook over low heat for 2 minutes, stirring constantly. Remove from heat; add vanilla and butter, stirring until butter melts. Cool

slightly; pour into cooled Gingersnap Crust. Garnish with whipped cream and pecans, if desired. Yield: one 9-inch pie.

GINGERSNAP CRUST:

1¼ cups gingersnap crumbs
1 tablespoon sugar
¼ cup butter or margarine, softened

Combine all ingredients in a small mixing bowl; blend well. Press firmly into a greased 9-inch piepan. Bake at 375° for 6 to 8 minutes or until set. Cool. Yield: one 9-inch pie crust.
Mrs. Toddie Lee Burns,
Canton, Tex.

FRESH PEACH COBBLER

¼ cup plus 2 tablespoons butter or margarine
2 cups sugar, divided
¾ cup all-purpose flour
2 teaspoons baking powder
Dash of salt
¾ cup milk
2 cups sliced peaches

Melt butter in a 2-quart baking dish. Combine 1 cup sugar, flour, baking powder, and salt; add milk and stir until mixed. Pour batter over butter in baking dish but do not stir.

Combine peaches and remaining 1 cup sugar; spoon over batter. Do not stir. Bake at 350° for 1 hour. Yield: 6 to 8 servings.
Mrs. Horace Edwards,
McCormick, S.C.

Chopped pecans and assorted fruits are baked in a cream cheese pound cake batter in Fruited Pound Cake (page 77).

Overleaf: Enjoy fresh, tender pods of okra—either Pickled Okra (page 8) or Creole Okra (page 99).

Vegetables and Side Dishes

Some people describe the South as one big vegetable garden; thus, it's no wonder that Southern cooks are known for their talent in cooking fresh vegetables. This chapter presents time-honored favorites like corn pudding and fried okra, as well as delicious new ways to enjoy the bounty.

Most fresh vegetables maintain their nutrients, color, and flavor when cooked quickly in a minimum amount of water. With the bright colors and distinctive flavors that vegetables add to the menu, your meals will never be ordinary.

SWEET-SOUR ASPARAGUS

2 tablespoons vegetable oil
2 tablespoons all-purpose flour
1 tablespoon brown sugar
¼ teaspoon salt
1½ tablespoons vinegar
⅛ teaspoon ground cinnamon
2½ cups cooked cut asparagus

Heat oil in a large skillet; add flour and stir until smooth. Add brown sugar, salt, vinegar, and cinnamon. Cover and cook until liquid is reduced about two-thirds. Add asparagus and simmer for 5 minutes. Yield: 6 servings.
Betty Ann Smith,
Orlando, Fla.

EASY BAKED BEANS

1 (16-ounce) can pork and beans
1 small onion, chopped
1 green pepper, chopped
1 teaspoon prepared mustard
1 teaspoon chili powder
3 tablespoons molasses
About ¼ cup catsup
2 slices bacon

Combine all ingredients except bacon. Pour into a 2-quart casserole. Place bacon on top. Bake, uncovered, about 40 minutes at 350°. Broil a few minutes to crisp bacon. Yield: 4 to 6 servings.
Verla Sullivan,
Nashville, Tenn.

MOLASSES BAKED BEANS

½ pound ground beef
2 (16-ounce) cans pork and beans
1 (15¾-ounce) can barbecue beans
1 medium onion, chopped
½ cup chopped green pepper
½ cup firmly packed brown sugar
¼ cup molasses
¼ cup catsup
2 tablespoons prepared mustard
1 tablespoon Worcestershire sauce
1 clove garlic, crushed
1 teaspoon seasoned salt
½ teaspoon lemon-pepper seasoning
4 or 5 slices bacon

Cook ground beef until browned; drain well.

Combine all ingredients except bacon in a mixing bowl; mix well and pour into a 13- x 9- x 2-inch baking dish. Top with bacon. Bake at 350° for 2 hours. Yield: 8 servings.

Mrs. Steve Toney,
Helena, Ark.

HOMEMADE PORK AND BEANS

1 pound dried navy or Great Northern beans
2 quarts water
¼ pound salt pork
¾ cup molasses
1 (6-ounce) can tomato paste
1 teaspoon salt
1 teaspoon dry mustard

Rinse beans in cold water and drain. Place in large saucepan and add water. Bring to a boil and boil 2 minutes. Remove from heat; cover loosely and let stand for 1 hour. (This takes the place of overnight soaking.) Return to heat and bring to a boil; cover and simmer gently over low heat for 1 hour or until beans are tender. Drain beans and reserve liquid.

Spoon beans into a 2½-quart beanpot or casserole. Cut through surface of salt pork every ½ inch, making cuts about 1 inch deep. Stir pork into beans. Mix 2 cups reserved bean liquid with molasses, tomato paste, salt, and mustard; pour over beans. Cover and bake at 300° for 5 to 6 hours. Check beans about once an hour and add additional hot bean liquid or water if beans become dry. At the beginning of cooking time, beans should be covered with liquid; at the end of the cooking time beans should be very moist and coated with a syrupy liquid. Yield: 8 servings.

CHILI BEANS

2 pounds dried pinto beans
2 pounds ground beef
1 large onion, finely chopped
1 (8-ounce) can tomato sauce
1 (16-ounce) can tomatoes
3 to 5 tablespoons chili powder
Salt to taste

Wash and sort beans; cover with cold water and soak overnight. The next day, heat to a boil; reduce heat and simmer 30 minutes. Add remaining ingredients and cook until beans are tender, about 1 hour. Stir often to prevent beans from sticking to pan. Yield: 12 to 16 servings.

Norma Kicklighter,
Greenville, S.C.

GREEN BEANS WITH ALMONDS

2 cups boiling water
¾ teaspoon salt
1 teaspoon sugar
2 pounds fresh green beans, cut or left whole
½ cup blanched, slivered almonds
¼ to ½ cup butter, melted

Combine water, salt, and sugar in a Dutch oven; bring to a boil. Add beans; cover and cook until barely tender (from 10 to 25 minutes). Drain, and place in serving dish.

Lightly sauté almonds in butter and sprinkle over green beans. Yield: 6 servings.

GREEN BEANS

2 pounds fresh green beans, cut into 1-inch
  pieces
3 cups boiling water
1 teaspoon salt
1 teaspoon sugar
2 slices bacon, quartered

Combine all ingredients in saucepan; bring to a boil over medium heat. Cover and simmer for 45 minutes to 1 hour or until tender; drain. Yield: 6 servings.

GREEN BEAN MARINADE

2 (15½-ounce) cans French-style green beans,
  drained
1 (16-ounce) can cut green beans, drained
1 (17-ounce) can English peas, drained
1 cup finely chopped celery
¼ cup chopped onion
1 medium-size green pepper, finely chopped
¼ cup chopped pimiento
¼ cup sliced water chestnuts
½ cup cider vinegar
½ cup vegetable oil
1¼ cups sugar

Combine first 8 ingredients. Combine vinegar, oil, and sugar; mix well. Pour over vegetables and toss gently to coat thoroughly. Refrigerate overnight. Drain well before serving. Yield: 8 servings.

GREEN BEANS SUPREME

1 pound fresh green beans, cut into 1-inch
  pieces
4 slices bacon
2 tablespoons bacon drippings
¼ cup chopped onion
1 (10¾-ounce) can cream of celery soup,
  undiluted
⅓ cup milk

Cook green beans in boiling salted water until tender; drain.

Fry bacon until crisp; drain and crumble. Sauté onion in bacon drippings until tender. Blend in soup, milk, and beans. Heat slowly, stirring occasionally. Place in serving dish; sprinkle bacon on top. Yield: 4 to 6 servings.

DEVILED BEETS

2 tablespoons vinegar
1 tablespoon brown sugar
1 tablespoon butter or margarine
1 teaspoon Worcestershire sauce
½ teaspoon salt
½ teaspoon paprika
¼ teaspoon dry mustard
¼ teaspoon ground cloves
3 cups diced, cooked beets

Combine all ingredients except beets in a medium saucepan; cook, stirring constantly, over low heat about 2 minutes. Stir in beets; cook about 4 minutes. Yield: 6 servings.
Sarah Dickerson,
Senatobia, Mo.

HONEY BEETS

1½ tablespoons cornstarch
½ teaspoon salt
2 tablespoons water
3 tablespoons vinegar
⅓ cup honey
2 tablespoons butter or margarine
2 cups sliced cooked beets

Combine cornstarch, salt, and water in a saucepan, stirring until blended. Add vinegar, honey, and butter; cook over medium heat, stirring constantly, until thickened. Add beets and cook until heated through, stirring constantly. Yield: 4 servings. *Lucille Hall,*
Bakersfield, Mo.

Tip: Freeze extra parsley in plastic bags; just snip off sprigs of frozen parsley as needed.

PICKLED BEETS

3 (16-ounce) cans small whole beets
2 cups sugar
2 cups water
2 cups vinegar
1 tablespoon mixed pickling spices
1 teaspoon ground cinnamon
1 teaspoon salt

Drain juice from 2 cans of beets. Place beets in a large bowl; add 1 can beets with juice. Set aside.

Combine remaining ingredients in a saucepan; cook until sugar melts. Pour over beets. Cover and refrigerate 4 to 8 hours. Yield: 8 servings.

Note: Reserve pickling juice for later use; drain additional beets before adding to juice.
Mattie Lou Patton,
Birmingham, Ala.

BRUSSELS SPROUTS PARISIENNE

2 tablespoons butter or margarine
2 tablespoons all-purpose flour
¼ teaspoon salt
⅛ teaspoon ground nutmeg
Dash of pepper
1 (13¾-ounce) can chicken broth
2 egg yolks, well beaten
¼ cup slivered almonds, toasted
1½ pounds fresh brussels sprouts or 2 (10-ounce) packages frozen brussels sprouts, cooked and drained

Melt butter in a 2-quart saucepan over low heat. Combine flour and seasonings; blend into butter, stirring constantly. Cook until mixture is smooth and bubbly. Remove from heat and stir in broth. Bring to a gentle boil, stirring constantly; boil 1 minute. Gradually add about one-fourth of mixture to egg yolks, stirring

constantly. Stir egg mixture into remaining hot mixture until well blended. Cook for 1 minute; stir in almonds and brussels sprouts. Cook until heated through. Yield: 6 to 8 servings.
Mrs. Gary Ferguson,
Dallas, Tex.

BROCCOLI-RICE CASSEROLE

1 (10-ounce) package frozen chopped broccoli
½ cup chopped onion
½ cup butter or margarine
1⅓ cups cooked rice
1 (8-ounce) jar process cheese spread
1 (10¾-ounce) can cream of mushroom soup, undiluted

Combine broccoli with onion and cook as directed on broccoli package; drain. Combine vegetables with remaining ingredients. Pour mixture into a greased shallow 2-quart casserole. Bake at 350° about 30 minutes. Yield: 6 to 8 servings.
Myra Musick,
Grapeland, Tex.

BROCCOLI WITH PIMIENTO-CHEESE SAUCE

2 (10-ounce) packages frozen broccoli spears
1 (10¾-ounce) can cream of mushroom soup, undiluted
½ cup butter or margarine, softened
1 tablespoon lemon juice
½ cup (2 ounces) shredded sharp Cheddar cheese
1 cup crushed cheese-flavored crackers
¼ cup slivered almonds or chopped pecans
1 (2-ounce) jar chopped pimiento

Cook broccoli according to package directions; arrange in buttered shallow 1½-quart casserole.

Combine soup, butter, lemon juice, and cheese; spoon over broccoli. Top with cracker crumbs, almonds, and pimiento. Bake at 350° for 20 minutes. Yield: 6 to 8 servings.
Myrtle Alvey,
Louisville, Ky.

CABBAGE SUPREME

1 medium cabbage
¼ cup butter
¼ cup all-purpose flour
½ teaspoon salt
¼ teaspoon pepper
2 cups milk
½ green pepper, chopped
½ medium onion, chopped
½ cup (2 ounces) shredded Cheddar cheese
½ cup mayonnaise
3 tablespoons chili sauce

Cut cabbage in small wedges and cook in boiling salted water until tender (about 15 minutes). Drain cabbage and place in a 13- x 9- x 2-inch casserole.

Melt butter in saucepan. Blend in flour, salt, and pepper. Cook over low heat, stirring constantly, until mixture is smooth and bubbly. Stir in milk and cook, stirring constantly, until smooth and thickened. Spread white sauce over cabbage in baking dish. Bake at 375° for 20 minutes.

Combine green pepper, onion, cheese, mayonnaise, and chili sauce. Spread over top of casserole and bake at 400° for an additional 20 minutes. Yield: 8 to 10 servings.

SKILLET CABBAGE

¼ cup bacon drippings
4 cups shredded cabbage
2 cups diced celery
2 large onions, sliced and separated into rings
2 tomatoes, chopped
1 green pepper, chopped
2 tablespoons sugar
¾ teaspoon salt
¼ teaspoon pepper

Heat electric skillet at 375° for 2 minutes; add bacon drippings and heat 1 minute. Add remaining ingredients; stir-fry about 5 minutes or until vegetables are crisp-tender. Yield: 6 to 8 servings. *Mrs. Steve Toney,*
Helena, Ark.

BAKED CREAMED CABBAGE

1 medium head cabbage, finely shredded
½ cup boiling salted water
3 tablespoons butter
3 tablespoons all-purpose flour
½ teaspoon salt
1½ cups milk
¼ cup breadcrumbs

Cook cabbage 9 minutes in boiling salted water. Drain cabbage well, and place in buttered 1½-quart casserole. Melt butter in saucepan; stir in flour and salt; cook over low heat 1 minute. Stir in milk gradually; cook over medium heat, stirring constantly, until thickened and bubbly. Pour sauce over cabbage and sprinkle breadcrumbs over top. Bake at 325° for about 15 minutes or until crumbs are browned. Yield: 6 servings.

EASY CABBAGE DISH

1 large cabbage, coarsely shredded
3 large tomatoes, sliced
1 large onion, sliced
1 large green pepper, sliced
1 cup chopped celery
3 tablespoons butter or margarine
1 tablespoon sugar
1 tablespoon salt
½ teaspoon pepper
¼ cup water

Combine all ingredients in a large skillet. Cover and simmer 30 minutes or until tender. Yield: about 10 to 12 servings.
Willie Sue Kelley,
Eldridge, Ala.

Tip: This is a handy method for freezing casseroles: line a casserole dish with heavy-duty aluminum foil, put the food in it, seal, and freeze. When the casserole is frozen, lift out the package, and mold foil to surface of food; seal securely with freezer tape, label, and return to the freezer.

COOL CARROTS

2 pounds carrots, peeled and sliced
1 green pepper, cut into rings
1 medium onion, thinly sliced and separated
    into rings
1 (10¾-ounce) can tomato soup, undiluted
1 cup sugar
½ cup vegetable oil
½ cup vinegar
1 tablespoon dry mustard

Cook carrots in boiling salted water 5 minutes or until crisp-tender. Drain.

Combine carrots, green pepper, and onion in a 13- x 9- x 2-inch pan; toss until mixed. Combine soup, sugar, oil, vinegar, and mustard; stir until combined. Pour soup mixture over carrot mixture. Cover; marinate in refrigerator 8 hours or overnight. Yield: 12 to 14 servings.
Edna Morgan,
Canton, Ga.

SPECIAL MINTED CARROTS

⅓ cup sliced water chestnuts
2 tablespoons margarine, melted and divided
2 cups cooked sliced carrots, drained
⅓ cup powdered sugar
1 teaspoon dried mint leaves or 1 tablespoon
    chopped fresh mint leaves
¼ teaspoon ground cinnamon

Sauté water chestnuts in 1 tablespoon margarine for 5 minutes; combine with carrots and place in a 1-quart casserole. Stir in remaining margarine.

Combine remaining ingredients; sprinkle over carrot mixture. Cover. Bake at 350° for 20 minutes, stirring frequently. Yield: 4 servings.
Eunice Palmer,
Morris Chapel, Tenn.

SWEET-AND-SOUR CARROTS

1 pound carrots, peeled and diagonally sliced
1 medium-size green pepper, chopped
⅓ cup sugar
1 teaspoon cornstarch
½ teaspoon salt
1 (8-ounce) can pineapple chunks
2 teaspoons vinegar
2 teaspoons soy sauce

Cook carrots, covered, in a small amount of boiling salted water until tender. Add green pepper; cook 3 minutes. Drain. Combine sugar, cornstarch, and salt in a medium saucepan. Drain pineapple and reserve juice. Add water to reserved pineapple juice to make ⅓ cup liquid; stir into sugar mixture. Stir in vinegar and soy sauce; cook over low heat until bubbly, stirring constantly. Stir in vegetables and pineapple; cook until heated throughout. Yield: 6 to 8 servings.
Mattye Holland,
Mineral Wells, Tex.

CAULIFLOWER WITH CHEESE SAUCE

1 teaspoon salt, divided
1 head cauliflower, broken into flowerets
2 tablespoons butter or margarine
2 tablespoons all-purpose flour
Dash of pepper
Dash of paprika (optional)
1 cup milk
1 cup (4 ounces) shredded Cheddar cheese
Fresh parsley sprigs (optional)

Bring 1 inch of water to a boil with ½ teaspoon salt in a medium saucepan; add cauliflower. Cover and cook 8 to 10 minutes, until crisp-tender. Drain and keep warm.

Melt butter in small saucepan over medium heat; add flour, ½ teaspoon salt, pepper, and paprika, if desired. Cook and stir 3 minutes or until bubbly. Gradually stir in milk; cook, stirring constantly, until smooth and thickened. Add cheese and stir until melted.

Arrange cauliflower on a platter and spoon

cheese sauce over top. Garnish with parsley, if desired. Yield: 6 to 8 servings.

Margaret Steele,
Jackson, Ky.

CELERY CASSEROLE

4 cups (1-inch-thick) celery pieces
1 (10¾-ounce) can cream of chicken soup, undiluted
¼ cup pimientos, diced
½ cup fresh breadcrumbs
¼ cup slivered almonds
2 tablespoons butter or margarine, melted

Cook celery in a small amount of boiling salted water about 8 minutes; drain. Combine celery, soup, and pimiento; spoon into a lightly greased 1-quart casserole.

Sprinkle breadcrumbs and almonds over celery mixture. Drizzle butter over top. Bake at 350° for 35 minutes. Yield: 4 to 6 servings.

NEW ORLEANS CORN PUDDING

¼ cup plus 2 tablespoons butter or margarine
2 tablespoons sugar
1 tablespoon plus 2 teaspoons all-purpose flour
½ cup half-and-half
4 eggs, well beaten
1½ teaspoons baking powder
3 pints or 2 (12-ounce) cans whole kernel corn, well drained
2 tablespoons brown sugar
¼ teaspoon ground cinnamon
2 tablespoons butter or margarine, melted

Heat butter with sugar in large saucepan until butter is melted. Stir in flour and mix well; remove from heat and gradually stir in half-and-half. Add eggs and baking powder; mix well. Add corn; mix well and spoon into a buttered 1½-quart casserole or soufflé dish. Bake at 350° for 45 minutes or until knife inserted in center comes out clean. Combine brown sugar and cinnamon. Drizzle melted butter over top of casserole; sprinkle with sugar mixture. Return to oven for about 5 minutes to brown. Yield: 6 to 8 servings.

EGGPLANT CASSEROLE

1 large eggplant, peeled and cut into ½-inch-thick slices
¼ cup butter or margarine, melted
Salt and pepper
1 medium onion, chopped
2 tablespoons vegetable oil
2 (8-ounce) cans tomato sauce
⅓ cup tomato paste
½ teaspoon dried oregano leaves
1 tablespoon chopped fresh parsley
1 egg, beaten
4 tablespoons grated Parmesan cheese, divided
1 cup cottage cheese

Place eggplant slices on a cookie sheet; brush with melted butter and sprinkle with salt and pepper. Broil 6 inches from broiler element for 5 minutes or until golden brown; turn slices over and broil until brown. Set aside.

Sauté onion in oil until tender. Add tomato sauce, tomato paste, oregano, and parsley; stir well. Set aside.

Combine egg, 2 tablespoons Parmesan cheese, and cottage cheese. Stir well and set aside.

Spoon half of tomato sauce mixture into a lightly greased 12- x 8- x 2-inch casserole dish. Arrange half of eggplant slices in tomato sauce. Spread cottage cheese mixture over eggplant. Top with remaining eggplant and remaining tomato sauce mixture. Sprinkle remaining 2 tablespoons Parmesan cheese over top of casserole. Bake at 350° for 40 minutes. Yield: 6 to 8 servings.

Anna Weber,
Atmore, Ala.

Tip: Cooking vegetables with the least amount of water possible will preserve vitamins and maintain flavor. Save the cooking liquid, and add to soup stock or gravy for additional food value and flavor.

PLEASANT HILL BAKED EGGPLANT

1 large eggplant
½ cup chopped onion
2 tablespoons butter
3 tablespoons chopped parsley
Dash of Worcestershire sauce
Salt and pepper to taste
1 (10¾-ounce) can cream of mushroom soup, undiluted
1 (8-ounce) package round buttery crackers, crushed
Butter

Wash eggplant and cut in half lengthwise. Scoop out pulp, leaving a ½-inch shell; set shells aside.

Chop pulp and cook in boiling salted water until tender; drain. Combine pulp and next 6 ingredients. Set aside ¼ cup cracker crumbs; add remaining crumbs to eggplant mixture.

Spoon filling into shells; sprinkle with reserved cracker crumbs and dot with butter. Place in a shallow baking pan; bake at 375° for 30 to 35 minutes. Yield: 6 servings.

SCALLOPED EGGPLANT

2 tablespoons chopped green pepper
2 tablespoons chopped onion
¼ cup butter or margarine, melted and divided
1 medium eggplant, peeled and cubed
2 cups chopped cooked or canned tomatoes
1 teaspoon salt
Dash of pepper
¾ cup bread cubes

Sauté green pepper and onion in 2 tablespoons butter. Add eggplant, tomatoes, salt, and pepper; cover and simmer 10 minutes. Spoon into a lightly greased 2-quart casserole.

Combine remaining butter with bread cubes; spoon over eggplant. Bake at 350° for 20 minutes or until eggplant is tender. Yield: 4 servings. *Mrs. James Barden,*
Suffolk, Va.

COLLARD GREENS WITH SALT PORK

1½ to 2 pounds fresh collard greens or 2 (10-ounce) packages frozen chopped collard greens
3 cups water
1½ teaspoons salt
½ cup diced salt pork

Examine leaves of collards carefully; remove pulpy stems and discolored spots on greens. Wash leaves thoroughly, drain well, and chop. Combine collards, water, and salt in a Dutch oven. Bring to a boil; reduce heat to low. Simmer, uncovered, for 25 minutes or until tender. Drain well. (Prepare frozen collard greens according to package directions.)

Cook salt pork in a skillet until golden brown; do not drain. Add collards, stirring lightly. Cook over low heat 5 minutes. Yield: 6 to 8 servings. *Edna Chadsey,*
Corpus Christi, Tex.

FRESH TURNIP GREENS

1 large bunch turnip greens (about 2 to 2½ pounds)
Salt
¼ pound salt pork, diced
About 3½ cups boiling water

Remove pulpy stems and discolored spots on greens. Wash thoroughly in several changes of warm water; add a little salt to the last water. Drain in colander.

Cook diced salt pork about 10 minutes in boiling water in covered saucepan. Add greens a few at a time; cover pot, and cook slowly for about 1 hour or until greens are tender. Do not overcook. Add additional salt, if needed. Yield: 6 servings.

Tip: For a quick way to peel tomatoes, hold tomato over flame or heat for 1 minute. You may prefer to dip tomato in boiling water for 1 minute, and then plunge it into cold water. The skin should slip off easily by either method.

[handwritten notes at top:]

Appetizers (to try)
Co. Living Recipes (Hardback)
Garden Cheese Dip (61)
Black-eyed Pea Cocktail Balls (63)
Cheese Rounds (62)
Cheddar Ball (61)
Orange almonds (63)
Crispy chicken sandwiches (64)
+ Turkey sausage Gumbo (96)
Subs. Turkey sausage
Progressive Farmer Co. Liv. Rec. 1988
Fried Red Tomatoes (106)
Jam Delights (106)
Squash Croquettes (104)
Herbed New Potatoes (101)
Skillet cabbage (95) oui

---

boiling salted water until tender, about 10 minutes. (Prepare frozen kale according to package directions.)

Melt 1 tablespoon butter in a small saucepan; stir in flour to make a smooth paste. Gradually stir in milk; cook over low heat, stirring constantly, until thickened. Set aside. Sauté onion in 2 tablespoons butter until tender. Stir in cooked kale.

Place half of kale mixture in a greased 2-quart baking dish. Arrange potato over kale; pour half of white sauce over potatoes. Spoon remaining kale mixture over sauce; pour remaining sauce evenly on top. Sprinkle cheese and breadcrumbs over sauce. Bake at 375° for 15 minutes. Garnish with egg slices. Yield: 6 to 8 servings.

Leslie Yambert,
Knoxville, Tenn.

STUFFED MUSHROOMS

1 pound fresh medium mushrooms
¼ cup butter or margarine
¼ cup chopped onion
¼ cup chopped celery
1 teaspoon Worcestershire sauce
½ teaspoon salt
⅛ teaspoon pepper
Butter or margarine, melted
¼ cup (1 ounce) shredded process American cheese

tly rinse mushrooms and pat dry. Rems and chop, reserving caps.

t butter in a skillet and add onion, nd mushroom stems; simmer until celder. Stir in Worcestershire sauce, salt, per.

sh mushroom caps with melted butter; vegetable mixture. Arrange mushrooms sed shallow baking dish. Sprinkle with Bake at 350° for 15 minutes or until s melted. Yield: 4 to 5 servings.

Mrs. W. P. Chambers,
Louisville, Ky.

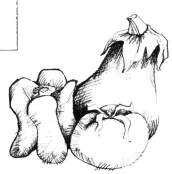

CREOLE OKRA

1 medium onion, sliced
1 medium-size green pepper, diced
1 small clove garlic, crushed
¼ cup bacon drippings
2 pounds okra, cut in ½-inch slices
4 medium tomatoes, peeled and chopped
1 teaspoon Worcestershire sauce
¼ teaspoon sugar
Salt
Pepper
1 teaspoon filé powder
Hot cooked rice

Sauté onion, green pepper, and garlic in bacon drippings in a Dutch oven until onion is tender. Add next 4 ingredients; salt and pepper to taste. Cover and cook over medium heat about 20 minutes. Remove from heat; stir in filé powder. Serve over rice. Yield: 8 servings.

Mrs. Harry H. Bock,
New Madrid, Mo.

OKRA AND TOMATOES

2 pounds okra
2 cups water
1 medium onion, sliced
1 tablespoon vinegar
1 teaspoon salt
2 tablespoons bacon drippings
1 (16-ounce) can stewed tomatoes
½ teaspoon sugar
½ teaspoon salt
⅛ teaspoon pepper

Wash okra well. Cut off tips and stem ends; cut okra crosswise into ½-inch slices.

Combine okra, water, onion, vinegar, and 1 teaspoon salt. Cover and cook over medium-high heat for 15 minutes. Drain; cook over low heat until all moisture evaporates. Add remaining ingredients; cook over medium heat, turning frequently, until brown. Yield: 6 to 8 servings. *C. Jobe, Tahlequah, Okla.*

OKRA SUPREME

2 medium potatoes, diced
5 cups sliced okra (about 1½ pounds)
½ cup cornmeal
½ cup vegetable oil
½ cup chopped green pepper or 1 banana pepper, chopped
2 tablespoons chopped onion
⅓ cup chopped bacon, uncooked
Salt and pepper to taste

Combine potatoes, okra, and cornmeal; mix well. Cook in hot oil in a large skillet until golden brown, stirring occasionally. Add remaining ingredients; stir well. Cover and cook about 5 minutes or until bacon is done. Serve hot. Yield: 8 servings. *Mrs. Marlene Miller, Trenton, Fla.*

Tip: Bake potatoes in half the usual time: let them stand in boiling water for 15 minutes before baking in a very hot oven.

FRITTER-FRIED OKRA

1 cup all-purpose flour
1 tablespoon baking powder
½ teaspoon salt
2 eggs, well beaten
⅓ cup milk
5 cups thinly sliced okra
Hot vegetable oil

Combine flour, baking powder, and salt in a medium mixing bowl; add eggs and milk, beating until smooth. Add okra, stirring until coated.

Spoon okra into hot oil in a large skillet; cook, stirring occasionally, until golden brown. Yield: about 6 servings. *Mrs. Steve Toney, Helena, Ark.*

PEAS COUNTRY STYLE

8 slices bacon
½ cup chopped onion
½ cup chopped green pepper
2 (16-ounce) cans English peas, drained
¼ cup chopped fresh parsley
1 teaspoon sugar
¼ teaspoon pepper

Fry bacon until crisp; crumble and set aside. Reserve 2 tablespoons bacon drippings in pan; sauté onion and green pepper in drippings until tender. Add remaining ingredients except bacon. Cover and cook over low heat 5 minutes, stirring occasionally. Garnish with bacon. Yield: about 6 servings. *Mrs. Max E. Ayer, Elizabethton, Tenn.*

BLACK-EYED PEAS

1 pound dried black-eyed peas
5 to 6 cups water
1 small ham hock
1 to 3 teaspoons salt
1 large onion

Wash and sort peas. Drain and place in heavy 6- to 8-quart kettle. Add water, cover, and soak 12 hours or overnight.

The next day, add ham hock to kettle (add more water if water does not cover peas) and bring to a boil. Reduce heat and add 1 teaspoon or more salt (start with a smaller amount if salty ham hock is used). Add whole onion. Cover and simmer about 1 hour or until peas are tender. To avoid excessive breaking of peas, do not stir during cooking. Add more salt if needed. Yield: 6 servings.

GOLDEN POTATO CASSEROLE

2 cups (8 ounces) shredded Cheddar cheese
¼ cup butter or margarine
2 (8-ounce) cartons commercial sour cream
⅓ cup chopped green onion
1 teaspoon salt
¼ teaspoon white pepper
6 medium potatoes, cooked in jackets, peeled, and coarsely shredded
2 tablespoons butter or margarine

Combine cheese and ¼ cup butter in a saucepan over low heat; stir until cheese is melted. Remove from heat; stir in sour cream, onion, salt, and pepper. Add potatoes, mixing gently. Pour into a buttered 2-quart casserole; dot with 2 tablespoons butter. Bake at 350° for 30 minutes. Yield: 8 to 10 servings.

Sandra E. Pratt,
Brownsville, Tenn.

SAVORY STUFFED POTATOES

6 medium baking potatoes
Butter or margarine
⅓ cup butter or margarine
½ cup milk
½ cup commercial sour cream
2 teaspoons salt
⅛ teaspoon pepper
2 tablespoons grated Parmesan cheese
Chopped chives

Wash potatoes and rub skins with butter. Bake at 425° for 1 hour or until done.

When cool to touch, slice skin away from top of each potato. Carefully scoop out pulp, leaving shells intact; mash pulp.

Combine potato pulp, ⅓ cup butter, milk, sour cream, salt, and pepper; beat with an electric mixer until smooth. Stuff shells with potato mixture; sprinkle each potato with cheese. Bake at 425° for 15 minutes. Sprinkle with chives and serve hot. Yield: 6 servings.

Mrs. R. J. Everhard,
Louisville, Ky.

FAT RASCALS

5 medium baking potatoes, grated
2 tablespoons all-purpose flour
5 tablespoons shredded Cheddar cheese
2 eggs, beaten
½ teaspoon salt
Dash of cayenne pepper
Vegetable oil

Combine all ingredients except oil in a large mixing bowl; mix well. Drain any liquid that accumulates.

Pour oil into a large skillet to the depth of ⅛ inch; heat oil to 350°. Drop potato mixture into hot oil, ¼ cup at a time; flatten slightly with a spatula, forming a circle. Cook 3 minutes on each side or until potatoes are browned. Add additional oil as necessary. Yield: 8 to 10 servings.

Marie Johnson,
Hamburg, Ark.

HERBED NEW POTATOES

1½ pounds new potatoes
¼ cup melted margarine
3 tablespoons chopped fresh parsley
1 tablespoon chopped fresh chives
1 tablespoon lemon juice
1½ teaspoons chopped fresh dill
Salt and pepper to taste

Pare a 1-inch strip around center of each potato. Cover potatoes and cook in boiling salted water for 25 minutes or until tender. Drain potatoes and set aside.

Combine remaining ingredients, stirring well. Pour over potatoes, coating thoroughly. Yield: 6 servings.

Carol T. Keith,
Fincastle, Va.

SWEET POTATO CASSEROLE

1 medium-size sweet potato, grated
1 (8¼-ounce) can crushed pineapple, undrained
½ cup raisins
½ cup sugar
1 teaspoon vanilla extract
½ teaspoon salt
½ cup milk
¼ cup butter or margarine, melted

Combine sweet potato, pineapple, raisins, sugar, vanilla, and salt in a medium mixing bowl; mix well. Spoon into a greased 8-inch square pan. Pour milk and butter evenly over sweet potato mixture. Bake at 350° for 45 to 50 minutes or until set. Yield: 4 servings.

Jane Crum,
North Little Rock, Ark.

MARMALADE-GLAZED SWEET POTATOES

6 sweet potatoes, boiled and peeled
1 (16-ounce) jar orange marmalade
2 tablespoons butter or margarine
3 tablespoons water
¼ teaspoon salt
Orange slices

Cut sweet potatoes lengthwise into 3 slices. (If small potatoes are used, cut in half.) Combine marmalade, butter, and water in a large skillet; bring mixture to a boil. Add potatoes and salt; cook over medium heat, turning frequently, until thoroughly glazed. Remove to serving platter and garnish with orange slices. Yield: 6 servings.

SWEET POTATO SOUFFLE

½ cup sugar
¼ cup butter or margarine, melted
½ cup light corn syrup
2 eggs
4 large sweet potatoes, cooked and mashed
Topping (recipe follows)

Combine sugar, butter, syrup, and eggs; beat until creamy. Stir in mashed sweet potatoes. Spoon mixture into a greased 2-quart baking dish and sprinkle with topping. Bake at 350° for 30 minutes. Yield: 6 to 8 servings.

TOPPING:

1 cup firmly packed light brown sugar
⅓ cup all-purpose flour
⅓ cup butter or margarine, melted
1 cup chopped pecans

Combine ingredients and mix well. Yield: about 2 cups.

Annette Smith,
Statesboro, Ga.

HOLIDAY YAMS

½ cup sugar
½ cup firmly packed brown sugar
2 tablespoons cornstarch
½ cup orange juice
¼ cup butter or margarine, melted
Salt to taste
4 or 5 medium yams or sweet potatoes, cooked, peeled, and sliced

Combine sugar and cornstarch; blend well. Stir in orange juice, butter, and salt. Simmer over low heat, stirring constantly, until slightly thickened.

Place yams in a lightly greased 2-quart casserole; add orange sauce. Bake at 350° for 30 minutes. Yield: 6 servings.

RUTABAGA-RICE CASSEROLE

2 cups cooked, mashed rutabaga
1 cup cooked regular rice
2 eggs, beaten
2 tablespoons butter or margarine
1 cup milk
1 tablespoon sugar
1 teaspoon salt
⅛ teaspoon ground nutmeg

Combine all ingredients in a large bowl; mix well. Spoon mixture into a buttered 10- x 6-

x 2-inch baking dish. Bake at 350° for 45 minutes. Yield: 8 servings. *Mrs. Marlene Miller, Trenton, Fla.*

SPINACH-MUSHROOM CASSEROLE

2 pounds fresh spinach
½ cup chopped onion
¼ cup butter or margarine, melted and divided
½ teaspoon salt
1 cup (4 ounces) shredded Cheddar cheese, divided
¼ pound small fresh mushrooms

Wash spinach thoroughly and drain; cook in a covered saucepan, without adding water, about 5 minutes or until tender, turning frequently. Drain well and chop coarsely.

Sauté onion in 2 tablespoons butter until tender; add spinach and salt, tossing gently. Spoon into a lightly greased 1-quart casserole; sprinkle with ½ cup cheese.

Sauté mushrooms in remaining 2 tablespoons butter; place on cheese. Sprinkle with remaining ½ cup cheese. Bake at 350° for 20 minutes. Yield: 6 servings. *Dolly Rivard, Petersburg, Ky.*

SPINACH SOUFFLE

2 tablespoons butter or margarine
2 tablespoons all-purpose flour
¾ cup milk
1 teaspoon chopped onion
1½ cups (6 ounces) shredded Cheddar cheese
3 eggs, separated
1½ cups chopped cooked spinach (about 1½ pounds uncooked)

Melt butter in a heavy saucepan over low heat; add flour, stirring until smooth. Cook 1 minute, stirring constantly. Gradually stir in milk; cook over medium heat, stirring constantly, until thickened and bubbly. Add onion and cheese, stirring until cheese melts. Beat egg yolks; stir a small amount of hot sauce mixture

into egg yolks, mixing well. Stir egg yolk mixture and spinach into sauce mixture.

Beat egg whites until stiff but not dry; fold into sauce mixture. Pour into a greased 1½-quart casserole; place casserole in a shallow baking pan. Fill pan 1 inch deep with water; bake at 350° for 45 to 50 minutes or until a knife inserted in center comes out clean. Yield: 8 servings. *Mrs. John A. Wyatt, Palmyra, Tenn.*

SPINACH SUPREME

2 pounds fresh spinach
¼ cup butter or margarine
3 tablespoons chopped onion
2 tablespoons all-purpose flour
½ cup evaporated milk
½ teaspoon garlic salt
⅛ teaspoon Worcestershire sauce
1 (6-ounce) roll process cheese food with jalapeño peppers
1½ tablespoons melted butter or margarine
½ cup dry breadcrumbs

Wash spinach thoroughly and drain; cook in a covered saucepan, without adding water, about 5 minutes or until tender, turning frequently. Drain well, reserving ½ cup liquid; chop coarsely.

Melt ¼ cup butter in a heavy saucepan over low heat; sauté onion until tender. Add flour, stirring until smooth. Cook 1 minute, stirring constantly. Gradually stir in milk and reserved spinach liquid; cook over medium heat, stirring constantly, until thickened and bubbly. Add garlic salt, Worcestershire sauce, and cheese, stirring until cheese melts. Add spinach; mix well. Spoon into serving dish. Stir 1½ tablespoons melted butter into breadcrumbs; sprinkle over top. Yield: 6 servings. *Mrs. Claudia Fowler, Baton Rouge, La.*

Tip: Keep bacon drippings in a covered container in the refrigerator; use for browning meats or seasoning vegetables.

SQUASH CASSEROLE

2 cups coarsely chopped cooked yellow squash
2 teaspoons instant minced onion
3 tablespoons butter or margarine, melted and divided
3 eggs, well beaten
Salt and pepper to taste
1 cup milk
1½ cups dry breadcrumbs, divided

Combine squash, onion, 1 tablespoon butter, eggs, salt, and pepper; blend well.

Pour milk over 1 cup breadcrumbs; set aside for 3 minutes. Stir into squash mixture. Spoon into a lightly greased 1-quart casserole.

Combine remaining breadcrumbs and butter; spoon over squash mixture. Bake at 350° for 30 minutes. Yield: 4 servings.

Carolyn McCareeth,
Oxford, Ala.

YELLOW SQUASH ST. TAMMANY

2 pounds yellow squash, sliced
Salt and pepper to taste
1 (10¾-ounce) can cream of chicken soup, undiluted
1 (2-ounce) jar diced pimiento, drained (optional)
2 carrots, shredded
1 small onion, chopped
1 (8-ounce) carton commercial sour cream
¼ cup butter or margarine, melted
1½ cups seasoned breadcrumbs

Cook squash in a small amount of boiling water until tender; drain well and mash.

Add salt and pepper. Combine soup, pimiento, carrots, onion, sour cream, and butter, blending well; add squash, stirring gently.

Alternate layers of squash mixture and breadcrumbs in a lightly greased 2-quart casserole. Bake at 350° for 30 minutes or until bubbly. Yield: 6 to 8 servings.

Tip: For best results in browning food in a skillet, dry the food first on paper towels.

FRIED SUMMER SQUASH

1 pound yellow squash, cut crosswise into ¼-inch slices
½ to ¾ cup cornmeal
Hot vegetable oil
Salt and pepper to taste

Dredge squash in cornmeal. Cook in 1-inch-deep hot oil until golden brown. Drain on paper towels and sprinkle with salt and pepper. Yield: 3 to 4 servings. *Mrs. Wesley Ford,*
Junction City, Ark.

SQUASH PATTIES

1 egg, beaten
1 tablespoon sugar
½ teaspoon salt
Dash of pepper
2 tablespoons milk
2 tablespoons finely chopped onion
1 cup cooked, mashed yellow squash
½ cup self-rising flour
Hot vegetable oil

Combine all ingredients except oil; mix well. Drop mixture by tablespoons into ⅛ inch hot oil in a large skillet. Flatten patties to ¼-inch thickness. Cook to golden brown; turn and brown on other side. Yield: about 14.

Dora McReynolds,
Lamar, Ark.

CHEESY SQUASH CASSEROLE

2 pounds small yellow squash, cut into 1-inch pieces
¼ cup plus 2 tablespoons butter or margarine, melted
1 teaspoon salt, divided
¼ cup plus 2 tablespoons all-purpose flour
2 cups milk
2 eggs, well beaten
2 cups (8 ounces) shredded sharp Cheddar cheese
½ teaspoon sugar
¼ teaspoon pepper
½ cup buttered breadcrumbs

Cook squash in boiling salted water to cover for 10 to 15 minutes or until tender. Drain well.

Combine butter, ½ teaspoon salt, and flour in a heavy saucepan; gradually add milk and cook over low heat, stirring constantly, until smooth and thickened. Stir about one-fourth of hot white sauce into eggs. Add squash, eggs, cheese, sugar, ½ teaspoon salt, and pepper to white sauce; cook over low heat, stirring constantly, for 5 minutes or until cheese melts. Pour into a deep greased 2-quart casserole. Sprinkle with breadcrumbs and bake at 375° for 40 minutes or until golden brown. Yield: 8 servings.

Betty Collier,
Fern Creek, Ky.

SQUASH MEDLEY

2 slices bacon, diced
1 medium onion, chopped
3 medium-size yellow squash, cut into ¼-inch slices
1 medium zucchini, cut into ¼-inch slices
2 medium tomatoes, cut into eighths
1 teaspoon salt
¼ teaspoon pepper
½ teaspoon dried basil leaves
½ teaspoon sugar

Fry bacon in large skillet until almost crisp. Add onion, squash, and tomatoes; sprinkle with remaining ingredients. Cover and cook over low heat 15 minutes, stirring several times. Yield: 5 to 6 servings.

Jane Crum,
North Little Rock, Ark.

HONEY-SPICED ACORN SQUASH

3 medium acorn squash
1 teaspoon salt
1 teaspoon ground ginger
¼ teaspoon ground nutmeg
¼ teaspoon pepper
3 tablespoons honey
2 tablespoons margarine, melted

Cut squash in half; scoop out and discard seeds. Place squash, cut side down, on a greased baking sheet. Bake at 375° for 30 minutes. Turn squash over.

Combine spices; add honey and margarine, stirring well. Brush squash with honey mixture; spoon remaining mixture into center of each squash. Bake 35 to 40 minutes longer or until squash is tender. Yield: 6 servings.

Mrs. Alfred Forbes,
Wagoner, Okla.

BAKED CUSHAW OR BUTTERNUT SQUASH

4 medium cushaw or butternut squash
⅔ cup firmly packed brown sugar
⅔ cup sugar
⅛ to ¼ teaspoon ground nutmeg
¼ teaspoon salt
4 teaspoons lemon juice
5 tablespoons butter

Wash, halve, and remove seeds from squash. Peel and cut into 1- to 1½-inch cubes (about 8 cups).

Combine all ingredients except butter in a lightly greased 3-quart casserole. Dot with butter. Cover with aluminum foil and bake at 375° for 45 minutes. Uncover and bake an additional 15 to 20 minutes or until squash is tender. Yield: 8 servings.

FRIED GREEN TOMATOES

4 large green tomatoes
½ cup all-purpose flour or cornmeal
1 teaspoon salt
¼ teaspoon pepper
Bacon drippings or vegetable oil

Cut tomatoes into ¼-inch slices. Combine flour, salt, and pepper; dredge tomato slices in flour mixture. Fry in hot bacon drippings until brown, turning once. Yield: 6 to 8 servings.

FRIED RED TOMATOES

1 tablespoon Dijon mustard
1½ teaspoons Worcestershire sauce
1 teaspoon sugar
½ teaspoon salt
¼ teaspoon paprika
Dash of red pepper
2 chilled tomatoes, cut into ½-inch slices
Cornmeal
Hot bacon drippings

Combine mustard, Worcestershire sauce, sugar, salt, paprika, and red pepper; stir well. Spread mixture onto both sides of tomato slices and coat with cornmeal. Sauté in about ¼-inch hot bacon drippings until lightly browned and crisp. Drain and serve hot. Yield: 4 servings.
Mrs. William B. Marks,
Harrisonburg, Va.

TOMATO DELIGHTS

6 firm, ripe tomatoes
Salt to taste
1 medium-size green pepper, chopped
1 small onion, chopped
¼ cup butter or margarine, melted
1 cup (4 ounces) shredded Cheddar cheese
1 cup cooked rice
1 egg, well beaten
¼ teaspoon dried oregano leaves
¼ teaspoon dried basil leaves
½ teaspoon salt
4 slices bacon, cooked and crumbled
Fresh parsley

Cut a slice from top of each tomato; scoop out pulp, leaving shells intact and reserving pulp. Sprinkle insides of tomato shells lightly with salt; invert to drain. Chop tomato pulp.
Sauté green pepper and onion in butter. Add remaining ingredients except parsley; stir well. Spoon into tomato shells and place in a shallow baking dish. Bake at 350° for 25 to 30 minutes. Garnish tomatoes with parsley. Yield: 6 servings.
Dorothy Adams,
Minden, La.

CRANBERRY SAUCE

2 cups sugar
2 cups water
4 cups fresh cranberries

Combine sugar and water; boil 5 minutes. Add cranberries; boil, without stirring, 10 to 20 minutes, depending on desired degree of thickness. Cool. Yield: about 4 cups.

CRANBERRY-ORANGE CHUTNEY

1 cup fresh orange sections
¼ cup orange juice
4 cups cranberries
2 cups sugar
1 cup chopped, unpeeled apple
½ cup raisins
¼ cup chopped walnuts
1 tablespoon vinegar
½ teaspoon ground ginger
½ teaspoon ground cinnamon

Combine all ingredients in a large saucepan, and bring to a boil. Reduce heat and simmer 5 minutes or until berries begin to burst. Chill until serving time. Yield: 5½ cups.

SPICED PEACHES

2 (29-ounce) cans cling peach halves
1⅓ cups sugar
1 cup cider vinegar
4 cinnamon sticks
2 teaspoons whole cloves

Drain peaches, reserving syrup. Combine peach syrup, sugar, vinegar, cinnamon sticks, and cloves in a saucepan. Bring mixture to a boil; then lower heat, and simmer 10 minutes. Pour hot syrup over peach halves; let cool. Chill thoroughly before serving. Store in refrigerator. Yield: about 4 pints.
Mildred Clute,
Marquez, Tex.

Home Entertaining Guide

Many people enjoy cooking but don't feel confident in planning menus. Others often cook for a crowd but never have room to seat them. And is there any way to avoid monotony in everyday meals?

The solutions to these problems and many more can be found within these pages. Entertaining is always fun and easy when you follow these guidelines, but don't be afraid to experiment with ideas of your own.

Building A Menu

Meal planning is a pleasure for some people, while for others it is a frustrating daily problem. Since a menu is more than just food, we offer some simple rules involved in planning foods for family and guest meals.

—*Do consider variety and nutrition.* It's important that meals be well balanced nutritionally and a variety of foods be served within the day.

—*Do think color.* Contrasts in color make an attractive plate. Balance a light-colored food with a red or green vegetable or salad. Even a sprinkling of paprika or a simple garnish can liven the appearance of food.

—*Do vary texture.* This can be accomplished by having some foods crunchy and some

foods smooth. Sometimes carrot or celery sticks or hard rolls are all that is needed to give crunch to a menu.

—*Do think flavor.* Plan flavor contrasts within a menu. Balance a spicy food with a bland one. Avoid serving more than one strong-flavored food. Condiments provide easy ways to introduce contrast in flavor.

—*Do consider temperature.* Serve hot things hot and cold things cold. Plan meals so that foods are at the right temperature when eaten. Consider seasonal temperatures, too. A congealed chicken salad is welcomed on a hot summer day, whereas a bowl of piping hot chili is more appropriate during cooler weather.

—*Do consider expendable time and energy.* Give thought to the simplicity or complexity of recipes, particularly when selecting them for a guest meal. Compose a menu which features some foods that can be prepared the day before. (Many salads and desserts lend themselves to early preparation.)

—*Do keep meals simple and don't overdo it.* Today a salad, main course, and dessert make a popular and well-rounded meal. Select recipes you are comfortable preparing for guests.

We have selected some everyday family menus, some that are suitable for special occasion dining, and some that are traditionally served on holidays. They are all designed to be flexible. Mix and match the recipes or make substitutions for your family's tastes. Be daring enough to make changes if in the smoked turkey menu you find a vegetable dish that you would like to use with your pot roast. In some cases it may be necessary to double a recipe or make two batches to meet your needs.

HEARTY BREAKFAST

Sunshine Shake *(page 17)*
Scrambled Eggs
Baked Country Ham *(page 40)*
Fat Rascals *(page 101)*
Fresh Fruit
Oatmeal Muffins *(page 25)*
Grape Jelly *(page 6)*
Coffee   Milk

WEEKEND BRUNCH

Tomato Juice Cocktail *(page 17)*
Family Fun Omelets *(page 39)*
or
Spinach-Egg Scramble *(page 39)*
Almond Swirl Ring *(page 30)*
or
Applesauce-Nut Bread *(page 27)*
Fresh Fruit
Coffee   Milk

SUNDAY NIGHT SUPPER

Open-Faced Chili Burgers *(page 18)*
Old-Fashioned Cabbage Salad *(page 58)*
Molasses Baked Beans *(page 92)*
Pickled Okra *(page 8)*
Peanut Butter Frosts *(page 80)*
or
Carrot-Orange Cookies *(page 78)*
Iced Tea   Coffee

SOUP AND SANDWICH SUPPER

Potato Soup *(page 64)*
Meatball Hero Sandwiches *(page 18)*
Ham-Stuffed Celery *(page 21)*
Vanilla Ice Cream
Blueberry Syrup *(page 84)*
Iced Tea   Coffee

FOURTH OF JULY BARBECUE

Barbecued Pork Shoulder *(page 42)*
Homemade Pork and Beans *(page 92)*
Broccoli and Cauliflower Salad *(page 58)*
Garlic Bread
Lemon Moist Cupcakes *(page 76)*
or
Homemade Strawberry Ice Cream *(page 81)*
Iced Tea   Lemonade

FIELD FEAST

Barbecued Beef and Pork Burgers *(page 17)*
Chili Beans *(page 92)*
Old-Fashioned Cabbage Salad *(page 58)*
Crisp Sweet Dill Pickles *(page 8)*
Chewy Fudge Brownies *(page 78)*
or
Apple Snack Cake *(page 74)*
Iced Tea

TAILGATE PICNIC

Buttermilk Chicken *(page 44)*
Marinated Vegetable Salad *(page 60)*
Molasses Baked Beans *(page 92)*
Sliced Tomatoes
Spiced Peaches *(page 106)*
French Rolls
Butter Pecan Cookies *(page 81)*
or
Watermelon
Lemonade

WEEKEND COOKOUT

Meat-Vegetable Kabobs *(page 38)*
or
Easy Shortribs *(page 38)*
Corn on the Cob
Peas Country Style *(page 100)*
Garden Glory Coleslaw *(page 58)*
French Bread
Vanilla Ice Cream Spectacular *(page 81)*
or
Fresh Apple Spice Cake *(page 73)*
Iced Tea   Lemonade

SUNDAY DINNER

Chicken Pot Pie *(page 45)*
or
Saucy Chuck Roast *(page 37)*
Squash Patties *(page 104)*
Green Beans *(page 93)*
Frosted Strawberry Salad *(page 55)*
or
Grapefruit Aspic *(page 53)*
Relish Tray
Hot Rolls
Raspberry Rhapsody *(page 82)*
Iced Tea

EASY OVEN MEAL

Meat and Cheese Loaf *(page 36)*
Broccoli-Rice Casserole *(page 94)*
New Orleans Corn Pudding *(page 97)*
or
Yellow Squash St. Tammany *(page 104)*
Vegetable Congealed Salad *(page 60)*
Hard Rolls
or
Oat-Molasses Bread *(page 31)*
Fresh Peach Cobbler *(page 88)*
or
Southern Gingerbread *(page 75)*
Iced Tea

COMPANY DINNER

Highland Pot Roast *(page 38)*
Spinach Supreme *(page 103)*
Fried Summer Squash *(page 104)*
Apricot Salad *(page 54)*
Never-Fail Pan Rolls *(page 32)*
Apple Crumb Pie *(page 85)*
Coffee

WILD GAME DINNER

Venison, Hunter's Style *(page 50)*
or
Saucy Doves *(page 49)*
Herbed New Potatoes *(page 101)*
Green Beans Supreme *(page 93)*
Honey-Spiced Acorn Squash *(page 105)*
Pickled Beets *(page 94)*
Hot Rolls
Deep-Dish Apple Pie *(page 85)*
or
Chocolate Meringue Pie *(page 86)*
Iced Tea   Coffee

FESTIVE THANKSGIVING DINNER

Hickory Smoked Turkey *(page 47)*

or

Smothered Quail *(page 50)*
Cornbread Dressing *(page 32)*
Golden Potato Casserole *(page 101)*
Green Beans With Almonds *(page 92)*
Cool Carrots *(page 96)*
Yellow Squash St. Tammany *(page 104)*
Cranberry Sauce *(page 106)*
Layered Holiday Salad *(page 55)*
Never-Fail Pan Rolls *(page 32)*
Creamy Coconut Cake *(page 75)*

or

Special Pecan Pie *(page 88)*
Iced Tea   Coffee

CHRISTMAS PARTY

Baked Country Ham *(page 40)*
Angel Biscuits *(page 31)*
Cheese Wafers *(page 19)*
Party O's *(page 20)*
Vegetable Dip *(page 21)*
Assorted Crackers
Glazed Pecans *(page 22)*
Fruited Pound Cake *(page 77)*
Hot Buttered Cranberry Punch *(page 16)*
Christmas Eggnog *(page 16)*

NEW YEAR'S LUNCH

Corn-Stuffed Pork Chops *(page 42)*
Black-Eyed Peas *(page 100)*
Fresh Turnip Greens *(page 98)*
Okra and Tomatoes *(page 100)*
Mexican Cornbread *(page 26)*
Egg Custard Pie *(page 86)*

or

Blueberry Yum-Yum *(page 82)*
Iced Tea

HOLIDAY FEAST

Crown Roast of Pork with Corn Stuffing
(page 43)
Marmalade-Glazed Sweet Potatoes *(page 102)*

or

Sweet Potato Soufflé *(page 102)*
Green Beans *(page 93)*
Cabbage Supreme *(page 95)*

or

Cauliflower With Cheese Sauce *(page 96)*
Cranberry Salad Supreme *(page 54)*
Relish Tray
Angel Biscuits *(page 31)*
Applesauce Fruit-Nut Cake *(page 74)*

or

Favorite Holiday Cake *(page 76)*
Iced Tea   Coffee

Table Settings

Setting an attractive table for family and guests is an exciting and rewarding aspect of meal planning. You need not have a formal dinner just to use your nicest tableware; every well-prepared meal deserves an attractive background. No longer need your best linens, china, silver, and crystal be reserved just for guests, but they should be enjoyed by your family as well.

To attain more variety in your table settings, begin by analyzing the table accessories you possess. Experiment mixing and matching colors of china, glassware, and linens for more excitement and individuality in setting your table. The addition of fresh flowers, fruit, autumn leaves, or candles may be all that you need to achieve a festive setting.

Traditional Table Setting

The traditional table setting is appropriate both for family meals and company dining. These suggestions are an easy guide to follow:

All flatware, napkins, and dishes are placed with the bottom edge 1 inch from the edge of the table. The flatware is arranged so that the pieces to be used first are farthest from the plate. The knife, cutting edge inward, should be placed to the right of the dinner plate; the fork or forks to the left. The teaspoon is placed to the right of the knife and the soup spoon to the right of it. A seafood fork is usually placed to the right of the teaspoon or soup spoon.

If the salad is to be served with the main course, the salad fork is placed to the left of the dinner fork; the salad plate is placed to the left of the forks.

The bread-and-butter plate is set at the tip of the forks. The butter spreader is placed across the top of the butter plate with the cutting edge toward the center of the plate.

The dessert fork or spoon may be on the table throughout the meal, or it may be brought to the table with the dessert. Another method is to place the dessert flatware (sometimes both a spoon and a fork) at the top of the place setting, parallel to the edge of the table, with the spoon handle going toward the right and the fork handle toward the left.

Water glasses are placed at the point of the knife and remain on the table throughout the meal. Wine glasses are set to the right of the water glass, and slightly forward, forming a diagonal line.

Traditionally, napkins are placed to the left of the forks, not under them. The edges of the napkin should be parallel to the forks and to the edge of the table. If the napkin has an embroidered initial or monogram, it should be folded so that the decorative design is in a legible position. The napkin may be placed in the center of the dinner plate, unless the first course is served before guests are seated.

Buffet Service

Buffet dinners or luncheons are a popular way to entertain and serve a large number of guests. They may be casual or elegant, and the menu may be simple or elaborate.

Buffets were once traditionally served from the sideboard in the dining room, but perhaps the greatest change in buffets is that the food has moved off the sideboard to the dining table and into many different rooms in the house. The surprise of being served in different rooms creates cheerful festivity while allowing guests to rotate more freely without crowding or lining up. Appetizers and dessert are particularly adaptable to serving in the garden room, den, or living room.

Traditional Table Setting

When setting up a buffet table, the prime consideration should be traffic flow. Placement should allow easy circulation before, during, or after the meal. Proximity to the kitchen is important so that serving dishes may be replenished with ease. The eye appeal of the table is also important when arranging the buffet. Food should be placed on the table in logical serving order: main dish, vegetables, salad, bread, and condiments. If the main dish is to be served over rice, the rice should come first in line. Salad dressings and sauces should be placed close to the dish they complement. Desserts may be served at one end of the buffet or placed on a serving cart and served after the guests have completed the main course. Beverages can be placed on a side table or served from a tray after the guests are seated.

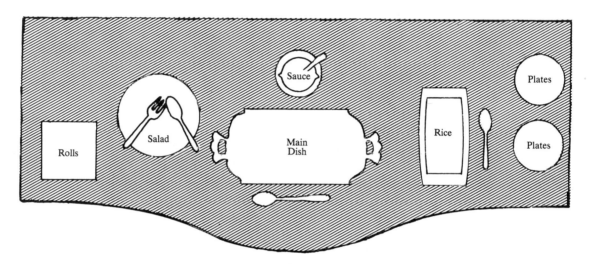

Buffet Served from a Sideboard

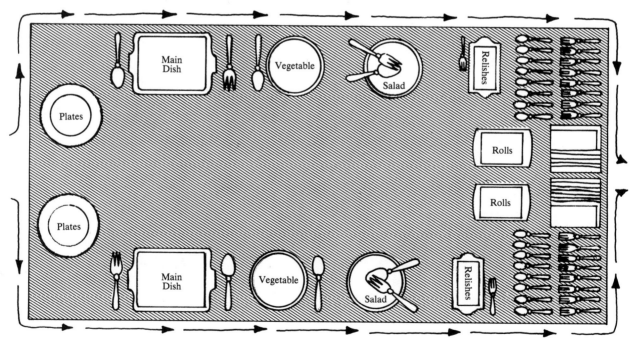

Duplicate Servings for a Large Buffet

When planning the arrangement of buffet service, consider what is convenient for you and your home. If the dining table is used as the serving table, it may be left in the center of the room or placed against the wall to provide additional space in a small room.

For a large crowd, the serving table is best placed in the center of the room with a serving line on each side of the table. With this arrangement two lines of guests may serve themselves at the same time.

For a seated buffet, the sideboard is perhaps most convenient for serving. The dining table may be set with everything except the dinner plates so that guests will have only their plates to carry through the buffet line. Or the dining table may be used for buffet service and small tables set up in the living room.

Cooking For A Crowd

In the South when folks gather for a special event, the homemade food plays a major role in the memories that linger. From church suppers and family reunions to christenings and birthdays, Southerners enjoy a feast and fellowship.

In preparing a meal for a large group, think before you panic. Good planning is essential to the success of an event. Here are some tips on organizing and serving a grand feast to avoid last minute crises.

—Make plans to accommodate everyone with comfortable seating.

—Plan the menu around familiar recipes; this is no time to experiment. Most recipes serve 4 to 6 and can easily be doubled to serve 8 to 12. To serve more than that, you will be much better off to cook in several moderate-size batches.

—Plan the arrangement of the table while you plan the menu to be sure of adequate space and tableware.

—Plan only one or two dishes that will need attention immediately before serving. Concentrate on dishes that can be prepared ahead.

—Note how many items are to be baked, and make sure you'll have adequate oven space. Plan for some foods to be cooked on the surface units. Also make use of electric skillets, toaster ovens, and warming trays for additional heating space.

—Refrigerator space will also be at a premium. Make sure you have enough shelf space for cold foods as well as for storage of foods prepared ahead. Turn the refrigerator to its coldest setting without freezing to compensate for the extra food.

—Be sure you have the proper cooking equipment and serving pieces for each dish on the menu.

—Do as many things ahead as possible. Cakes, pies, cookies, breads, and some casseroles and sauces can be prepared in advance and frozen until needed. Salad dressings, gelatin salads, and desserts can generally be made one or two days in advance.

—On the day of the dinner, set the table early in the day. You can also unmold gelatin salads early and refrigerate until serving time, as well as cut some cakes and pies.

—Organize serving and cleaning up so that guests can help themselves and later deposit plates at dishwasher or waste can to reduce clutter and save time.

Appendices

EQUIVALENT WEIGHTS AND MEASURES

Food	Weight or Count	Measure or Yield
Apples	1 pound (3 medium)	3 cups sliced
Bacon	8 slices cooked	½ cup crumbled
Bananas	1 pound (3 medium)	2½ cups sliced, or about 2 cups mashed
Bread	1 pound	12 to 16 slices
Bread	About 1½ slices	1 cup soft crumbs
Butter or margarine	1 pound	2 cups
Butter or margarine	¼ - pound stick	½ cup
Butter or margarine	Size of an egg	About ¼ cup
Cabbage	1 pound head	4½ cups shredded
Candied fruit or peels	½ pound	1¼ cups cut
Carrots	1 pound	3 cups shredded
Cheese, American or Cheddar	1 pound	About 4 cups shredded
cottage	1 pound	2 cups
cream	3 - ounce package	6 tablespoons
Chocolate morsels	6 - ounce package	1 cup
Cocoa	1 pound	4 cups
Coconut, flaked or shredded	1 pound	5 cups
Coffee	1 pound	80 tablespoons (40 cups perked)
Corn	2 medium ears	1 cup kernels
Cornmeal	1 pound	3 cups
Crab, in shell	1 pound	¾ to 1 cup flaked
Crackers		
chocolate wafers	19 wafers	1 cup crumbs
graham crackers	14 squares	1 cup fine crumbs
saltine crackers	28 crackers	1 cup finely crushed
vanilla wafers	22 wafers	1 cup finely crushed
Cream, whipping	1 cup (½ pint)	2 cups whipped
Dates, pitted	1 pound	3 cups chopped
Dates, pitted	8 - ounce package	1½ cups chopped
Eggs	5 large	1 cup
whites	8 to 11	1 cup
yolks	12 to 14	1 cup
Flour		
all-purpose	1 pound	3½ cups
cake	1 pound	4¾ to 5 cups sifted
whole wheat	1 pound	3½ cups unsifted
Green pepper	1 large	1 cup diced
Lemon	1 medium	2 to 3 tablespoons juice and 2 teaspoons grated rind
Lettuce	1 pound head	6¼ cups torn
Lime	1 medium	1½ to 2 tablespoons juice
Macaroni	4 ounces (1 cup)	2¼ cups cooked
Marshmallows	11 large	1 cup
	10 miniature	1 large marshmallow
Marshmallows, miniature	½ pound	4½ cups

Food	Weight or Count	Measure or Yield
Milk		
evaporated	5.33 - ounce can	⅔ cup
evaporated	13 - ounce can	1⅝ cups
sweetened condensed	14 - ounce can	1¼ cups
sweetened condensed	15 - ounce can	1⅓ cups
Mushrooms	3 cups raw (8 ounces)	1 cup sliced cooked
Nuts		
almonds	1 pound	1 to 1¾ cups nutmeats
	1 pound shelled	3½ cups nutmeats
peanuts	1 pound	2¼ cups nutmeats
	1 pound shelled	3 cups
pecans	1 pound	2¼ cups nutmeats
	1 pound shelled	4 cups
walnuts	1 pound	1⅔ cups nutmeats
	1 pound shelled	4 cups
Oats, quick-cooking	1 cup	1¾ cups cooked
Onion	1 medium	½ cup chopped
Orange	1 medium	⅓ cup juice and 2 tablespoons grated rind
Peaches	4 medium	2 cups sliced
Pears	4 medium	2 cups sliced
Potatoes, white	3 medium	2 cups cubed cooked or 1¾ cups mashed
sweet	3 medium	3 cups sliced
Raisins, seedless	1 pound	3 cups
Rice, long-grain	1 cup	3 to 4 cups cooked
pre-cooked	1 cup	2 cups cooked
Shrimp, raw in shell	1½ pounds	2 cups (¾ pound) cleaned, cooked
Spaghetti	7 ounces	About 4 cups cooked
Strawberries	1 quart	4 cups sliced
Sugar		
brown	1 pound	2¼ cups firmly packed
powdered	1 pound	3½ cups unsifted
granulated	1 pound	2 cups
Whipping cream	1 cup	2 cups whipped

METRIC CONVERSION CHART

When You Know . . .	Approximate Conversion to Metric Measures		
	Multiply by . . .	To Find . . .	Symbol
	Mass (weight)		
ounces	28	grams	g
pounds	0.45	kilograms	kg
	Volume		
teaspoons	5	milliliters	ml
tablespoons	15	milliliters	ml
fluid ounces	30	milliliters	ml
cups	0.24	liters	l
pints	0.47	liters	l
quarts	0.95	liters	l
gallons	3.8	liters	l

Fahrenheit to Celsius: Subtract 32 • Multiply by 5 • Divide by 9
Celsius to Fahrenheit: Multiply by 9 • Divide by 5 • Add 32

EQUIVALENT MEASUREMENTS

Use standard measuring cups (both dry and liquid measure) and measuring spoons when measuring ingredients. All measurements given below are level.

3 teaspoons	1 tablespoon
4 tablespoons	¼ cup
5⅓ tablespoons	⅓ cup
8 tablespoons	½ cup
16 tablespoons	1 cup
2 tablespoons (liquid)	1 ounce
1 cup	8 fluid ounces
2 cups	1 pint (16 fluid ounces)
4 cups	1 quart
4 quarts	1 gallon
⅛ cup	2 tablespoons
⅓ cup	5 tablespoons plus 1 teaspoon
⅔ cup	10 tablespoons plus 2 teaspoons
¾ cup	12 tablespoons
Few grains (or dash)	Less than ⅛ teaspoon
Pinch	As much as can be taken between tip of finger and thumb

HANDY SUBSTITUTIONS

Even the best of cooks occasionally runs out of an ingredient she needs and is unable to stop what she is doing to go to the store. At times like those, sometimes another ingredient or combination of ingredients can be used. Here is a list of substitutions and equivalents that yield satisfactory results in most cases.

Ingredient Called For	Substitution
1 cup self-rising flour	1 cup all-purpose flour plus 1 teaspoon baking powder and ½ teaspoon salt
1 cup cake flour	1 cup sifted all-purpose flour minus 2 tablespoons
1 cup all-purpose flour	1 cup cake flour plus 2 tablespoons
1 teaspoon baking powder	½ teaspoon cream of tartar plus ¼ teaspoon soda
1 tablespoon cornstarch or arrowroot	2 tablespoons all-purpose flour
1 tablespoon tapioca	1½ tablespoons all-purpose flour
2 large eggs	3 small eggs
1 egg	2 egg yolks (for custard)
1 egg	2 egg yolks plus 1 tablespoon water (for cookies)
1 cup commercial sour cream	1 tablespoon lemon juice plus evaporated milk to equal 1 cup; or 3 tablespoons butter plus ⅞ cup sour milk
1 cup yogurt	1 cup buttermilk or sour milk
1 cup sour milk or buttermilk	1 tablespoon vinegar or lemon juice plus sweet milk to equal 1 cup
1 cup fresh milk	½ cup evaporated milk plus ½ cup water
1 cup fresh milk	3 to 5 tablespoons nonfat dry milk solids in 1 cup water
1 cup honey	1¼ cups sugar plus ¼ cup liquid
1 square (1 ounce) unsweetened chocolate	3 tablespoons cocoa plus 1 tablespoon butter or margarine
1 clove fresh garlic	1 teaspoon garlic salt or ⅛ teaspoon garlic powder
1 teaspoon onion powder	2 teaspoons minced onion
1 tablespoon fresh herbs	1 teaspoon dried herbs or ¼ teaspoon powdered herbs
¼ cup chopped fresh parsley	1 tablespoon dehydrated parsley
1 teaspoon dry mustard	1 tablespoon prepared mustard
1 pound fresh mushrooms	6 ounces canned mushrooms

Index